SCHOLASTIC

YOU CAN

Motivate reluctant readers

Kate Ruttle

FOR AGES 7-11

"Reluctant readers can sometimes read very well but are not motivated..."
('Reading for Purpose and Pleasure', Ofsted)

Credits

Author
Kate Ruttle

Development Editor
Kate Pedlar

Project Editor
Fabia Lewis

Series Designer
Catherine Perera

Cover Designer
Anna Oliwa

Cover photography
© Ingram Publishing/Superstock

Design
Q2A Media

Designed using Adobe InDesign

Published by Scholastic Ltd
Villiers House
Clarendon Avenue
Leamington Spa
Warwickshire CV32 5PR

www.scholastic.co.uk

Printed by Bell and Bain Ltd.
1 2 3 4 5 6 7 8 9 9 0 1 2 3 4 5 6 7 8

British Library Cataloguing-in-Publication Data
A catalogue record for this book is available from the British Library.
ISBN 978-1407-10174-3

Contents

Contents

Introduction

Reading is the most important skill that we teach children in primary school. Even by the time children are seven, their access to much of the curriculum will diminish if they can't read, and as they move up through Key Stage 2 the consequences of not being able to read will increase. Secondary school teachers are generally less well-trained in teaching reading than their primary school colleagues, and secondary school children are much less tolerant of non-readers than their primary counterparts. So if you have reluctant readers in your class, it is important to do everything you can to help them now.

Identifying the barriers to learning

The first task is to identify the barriers: is there a problem with attitude, with sight, with learning, with experience…? This book helps you to establish what the problems may be by suggesting some simple questions you can ask and by providing some classroom screening procedures – including one that explores whether or not it might be worthwhile asking for a dyslexia screen. Thereafter, the book falls roughly into two parts.

Teaching skills for reading

By the time reluctant readers are seven and over, their belief in themselves as poor readers is becoming set, so it is sometimes useful to teach key skills through contexts other than books. Fortunately, primary school teachers are generally skilled in thinking laterally and in recognising ways in which skills can be taught and later applied to improve reading, which ultimately increases children's opportunities to learn to read without putting them at risk of failure.

Practising skills for reading

In Key Stage 2, many of the children who *can* read, as well as those who *could* read if they chose to make the effort, will do better if they have a clear, exciting reason for reading. This book includes ideas for treasure hunts, for poetry awards, for book quizzes; it acknowledges the power of film and TV as well as computer games and the internet; it includes ideas to give children the tools they need to become readers in different contexts.

Throughout the book you will find ideas: some of which will be familiar or a twist on a familiar idea and some of which will probably be new to you. The ideas are all tried and tested in Key Stage 2 classrooms and all have been used to engage reluctant readers. Use them, adapt them and develop from them strategies and activities that will work in your classroom to help to ensure that you can motivate your reluctant readers.

You Can... Explore reasons for reluctance to read

Before you can help the 'reluctant readers' in your class it is important to try to establish why they are reluctant: different problems require different solutions. If you have more than one reluctant reader in your class make sure you think about them individually while you consider how best to help them, as they may be encountering very different obstacles in reading.

Thinking points

● What is it that makes you think of a child as a 'reluctant reader'? Are you looking at a child who is always happy and cheerful – apart from when asked to read? Is this a child who is doing well in maths but is making poor progress in reading? Does the child use strategies to avoid drawing attention to his or her reading ability such as hiding their reading book or chatting to their neighbour instead of completing their spelling worksheet?

● Reasons for a child's reluctance to read are diverse and may relate to their home background, their own self-perception, their interest in reading or their overall maturity. It may also be the result (not the cause) of a reading difficulty.

Tips, ideas and activities

● Complete the photocopiable 'Child's profile' on page 56 as a starting point: there might be a problem which is causing the reluctance to read.

● Discuss with parents and other members of staff whether or not there is any history of reading problems in the child's family. If so, try to find out as much as you can about these: what were the causes? How did any older siblings overcome their reluctance to read?

● There may be difficulties around processing language and this is not an uncommon problem, even at Key Stage 2. If the child's language processing skills are poor, then their ability to understand text will be affected and this may impact on their motivation and interest.

● It is possible that the child hasn't yet been motivated to read because they've never come across a text that has interested them. Try to present as wide a variety of books as possible to the child, including both fiction and non-fiction, comics, TV-related books, puzzle books, catalogues and interactive books. If you can find something to grab the child's interest, you can build on this.

● Try to interest the child in non-fiction books. Many children, in particular boys, are more interested in non-fiction than in stories. There are many excellent non-fiction books available as part of reading schemes, so if a child is interested in non-fiction rather than fiction this no longer needs to hinder their progress in reading.

● Watch the child's reactions when you read fictional texts aloud. Does the child listen attentively – or at least listen? Can they discuss stories, express opinions about events and participate in related drama activities? Or does the lack of interest in reading extend to stories?

You Can... Explore reasons for reading difficulties

Is your reluctant reader unwilling to read, or do they have difficulties? By the time they are in Key Stage 2, many children who experience difficulties will try to disguise them – and children have a surprising number of strategies for diverting your attention from the fact that they simply can't read. So if there are reading difficulties, what can you do about them?

Thinking points

● Reaching Key Stage 2 without being able to read well is a cross-curricular disadvantage as reading is at the heart of almost every subject.

● Children of this age are very often reluctant to admit they can't do something – especially something that their peers can do. This puts particular pressure on your relationship with the child because in order for you to do any kind of intervention, the child needs to know that they can trust you. Allowing themselves to be involved in an intervention is a tacit admission that there is a problem. Diagnosing the problem is therefore a very delicate process as you must not imply that the child is failing, while at the same time you need to find out what the child can't do – and why.

Tips, ideas and activities

● Start off by investigating the obvious, using the record form on photocopiable page 56. Establish if there is a vision or hearing problem; even if the child has never complained of either, try getting them checked. Children who have always had a problem with sight or hearing don't know that there is another way for it to be.

● Compare the child's attainment across the curriculum. If it is uniformly low then reading itself is unlikely to be the root cause of the problem. If this is the case you need to consider the child's progress as a whole and plan the route forwards in small, manageable steps.

● Use the photocopiable sheets 'Phonological awareness MOT' on page 57 and 'Behaviours associated with dyslexia' on page 58. If the child has poor phonological processing together with a poor short-term memory, then ask for a dyslexia screen.

● Is there a problem with concentration and attention? Consider other comparable children in the class – and your experience of teaching this age group. Time how long the child is able to focus on a reading task, compared to other tasks in the classroom.

● Does the child have difficulty *comprehending* rather than *decoding*? If a child is not making meaning, it could be that they went through the early stages of a reading scheme too fast, with an emphasis on decoding, and have never acquired the habit of making meaning; or it could be that they are now reading books that are too difficult for them to both decode and make meaning. Either way, try an easier book and see if you can kick-start their comprehension of texts.

● The principles of assessment for learning are particularly important when working to overcome a child's reluctance to read: establish where the child is, and where they want to be and then plan the steps to bridge the gap. Remember the importance of small steps: even when you manage to work out what the sticking point is, the child is not likely to make a miraculous leap forwards.

You Can... **Ensure phonic strategies**

Some children in Key Stage 2 may be playing catch up with their phonic knowledge. If they have not been taught phonics systematically in Key Stage 1 – or if they weren't ready to benefit from the instruction they received – there may be holes in their knowledge. If children of this age are reluctant to read, there is a good chance that they are struggling to some extent. It's worth doing a quick phonics MOT just to check that phonological awareness isn't holding them back.

Thinking points

● Children who are struggling to read in Key Stage 2 may well be labelled as dyslexic by anxious parents. The British Dyslexia Association estimates that about ten per cent of the population are dyslexic, with about four per cent being sufficiently dyslexic for it to cause them problems in reading and writing development.

● Poor short-term memory together with poor phonological awareness are key indicators for dyslexia. Dyslexic children also find sequencing activities difficult and are often poorly organised. If you are concerned, it may be worth asking your SENCO for a dyslexia screen.

Tips, ideas and activities

● A phonological awareness MOT can include the following activity types, supported by pictures or objects, to ensure that memory isn't impeding phonological processing. (See page 57 for a record sheet.)

● Check that children can orally segment words into phonemes, for example, coin, *c-oi-n*; stamp, *s-t-a-m-p*.

● Using picture cards, ask children to tell you what the new word would be if you:
  ● Changed the initial letter.
  ● Changed the final letter.
  ● Omitted one of two adjacent consonants.

● Can children tell you what the new word would be if you changed letters in a CCVC word? Do this activity orally, for example, say *pray* and then change the *r* to *l* and ask children to say the new word.

● Give children one picture and ask them to find a rhyme from a set of three others:
  ● Include a decoy that begins with the same sound as the initial word, for example, *spade, spoon*.
  ● Include a decoy that is associated with the initial word, for example, *spade, sand*.
  ● Have one picture that rhymes, for example, *spade, wade*.

● Can children tell you the odd one out of three or four words? Ask questions like:
  ● *Listen to these three words. Which one begins with a different sound?*
  ● *Which one doesn't rhyme?*
  ● *Which one has a different end sound?*
  ● *Which one has a different middle sound?*

You Can... **Check high-frequency words**

Many of the most commonly occurring words in English are spelled in idiosyncratic ways, which are neither predictable nor decodable. It helps children to make sense of a text as they read if they are able to read these words automatically and with instant recognition. No matter what other strategies they are using, if children can't recognise these words, making meaning while reading will be a problem.

Thinking points

● If you receive children in your class who have been trained to decode text well, you may have fewer problems with children not recognising high-frequency words – but you may have some children who use phonics to extremes and try to plough on through the word, pronouncing it as they feel it should be pronounced and failing to make any meaning.

● The current orthodoxy is to divide high-frequency words into 'decodable' and 'tricky': but that only applies if children know what the words say and they can make a judgement about whether or not their spelling is irregular. As a reader, these are words that need to be recognised by sight in any context and in any font.

Tips, ideas and activities

● Play games to teach the words.
  ○ Let pairs of children regularly make their own games of *Lotto* and *Snap!* and make opportunities for children to play the games at odd times during the day. Challenge them to complete an entire game within five minutes, four minutes, three minutes and so on.
  ○ Make a 5 x 5 grid. Write three different high-frequency words in spaces in the grid and fill the rest of the cells with a variety of decoy words. (Refer to the synthetic phonics scheme, *Letters and Sounds* (DfES, 2007) for lists of appropriate high-frequency words.) Time children as they scan the grid for the three high-frequency words. As children become better, add more cells and more high-frequency words. Keep asking children to find them more quickly so that the words are over-learned and are recognised automatically.
  ○ Ask children to colour shapes on squared paper to show the outline of a word, for example, *was* as a three-square flat word; *said* as four squares in a row with an ascender at the end; *could* and *would* have similar shapes, but *should* is quite different. Ask them to match the word to the shape. Then ask them just to 'read' the shape.
  ○ It may be necessary to re-teach children to look at a bigger shape than individual letters and letter patterns. Try making a mask (a postcard-sized piece of card with a word-sized slit in the middle). Move the card over text, pausing every now and again and ask a child to quickly say the word they can see. Don't use this for reading, but just for individual word recognition.

● All of these games and activities need to be followed up by authentic reading experiences. Before you ask a child to read, ask them to scan the text for any words they have been practising. If they can't recognise the word immediately, continue to practise it through games, flashcards and other activities.

You Can... **Teach word structure**

In order for children to become proficient readers, they need to learn to move away from the easy single syllable and phonically decodable words and their reliance on supportive illustrations, which are often hallmarks of initial reading books. Children who lack confidence can quickly learn to avoid those longer words which they find intimidating. Teaching reluctant readers some strategies for breaking down a longer word can be an important breakthrough.

Thinking points

● One of the key strategies that teachers tend to teach children is to break a word into syllables. But what is a syllable? Many an academic has spent hours debating this question and yet it's one which we expect children to solve with comparatively little support. One useful definition of a syllable is 'a vowel phoneme and its surrounding consonants'. All syllables have to have a vowel phoneme, and most also have consonants, although it's not a requirement (think of the first syllable in *a-bout*).

● Don't spend time debating exactly where the syllable boundary lies in a word. As long as the child can use the syllable boundaries to support their reading of the word, it's not particularly important whether they want to draw the boundary at, for example, *ra-bbit, rab-bit* or *rabb-it*.

Tips, ideas and activities

● Check, first of all, that children can count the syllables in a long word. Since animal names are a rich source of multi-syllabic words, it's a comparatively easy activity to set up a 'zoo' and ask children to sort animals into zones depending on the number of syllables in their names. Do this activity orally at first.

● Once children have sorted animals' names orally, let them see the names and work out strategies for reading them.

● Cut the words into syllables.

● Use music sessions to explore the stress patterns in words. A lot of words in English have unstressed first syllables, and changing the stress around in a word can make it sound quite different. Practise playing with the stress patterns in words by varying the stressed syllables for example, **im**-*por-tant*; *im-**por**-tant*; *im-por-**tant*** and listening to the impact on the vowel phonemes. It's sometimes the case that shifting the stress can make an implausible word into a recognisable one. Near homophones (for example, *bellow* and *below*) can also be untangled through shifting the stress.

● Teach children how compound words are constructed. Introduce the idea that some compounds are completely joined, for example, *hairbrush*, some are partially joined, for example, *lamp-post* and others are just adjacent words, for example, *light bulb*. If children are aware of compound words, they can often decipher longer words by breaking them down into shorter, more familiar words.

● Give children practice in recognising prefixes and suffixes. A lot of the vocabulary in English has the potential for having prefixes and suffixes added on to it, even though they are used less in children's spoken English. Again, if children recognise common suffixes and prefixes, this can remove some of the panic that sets in when they are faced with longer words.

You Can... **Teach reading for meaning**

It is important to insist that children make meaning when they are reading. The earlier that children understand that reading must make meaning, the more likely they are both to enjoy reading and to develop good reading habits. Children who 'bark' inaccurately at print are very likely to develop into reluctant readers since reading quickly becomes a meaningless chore. Your reluctant readers should be encouraged to engage with reading challenges which emphasise the importance of making meaning when reading.

Thinking points

● Do your children know that writing is intended to communicate meaning? Have you explicitly discussed with them the idea that writers write books in order to share their ideas and stories? These facts may seem obvious to competent adult readers, but are a revelation to many young readers.

● Introduce your children to the authors and illustrators of books – many publishers and authors have pictures and interviews on websites and these can be a powerful motivator for persuading children to read since they may then understand that the point of reading is to find out what the author has chosen to communicate to them.

Tips, ideas and activities

● When you listen to children reading, insist on their reading making sense. Inaccuracies which keep the sense can be allowed until a page or book is finished; those that lose the meaning should be corrected before moving on. Teach children to take responsibility for self-monitoring so that they know when they lose meaning and take action to repair it.

● Encourage children to write for each other. Set up part of your classroom book corner so you make children's own work available to be read by others. Invite the 'authors' to read their own work to their friends and encourage all children to read each other's work.

● Make simple treasure hunts around the classroom or introduce orienteering trails around the school and playground. The treasure hunts/trails should consist of clues which need to be read in order to find an answer.

● Boys who are reluctant to read may well enjoy solving puzzles and challenges. Write your own simple texts for them, including a word in each sentence which shouldn't be there because it doesn't make sense. Challenge children to find and delete the word. This type of activity helps to keep children interested when their skills are beginning to plateau.

● Recognise the lure of the computer. Allow children to do reading activities on-screen. This can include developing their own text using wordbanks, editing and improving typed text and purposeful reading when they complete activities and play games.

● Allow children to read non-fiction books about topics that interest them. Non-fiction is often easier to read than fiction because you don't have to remember events from the beginning of the book in order to make sense of the text – facts tend to be short and self-contained. Let children become 'class experts', expecting them to research and find the answers to each others' questions.

You Can... **Teach punctuation**

Ask your children what they think punctuation is for. Many children think that the reason writing is punctuated is so that the reader knows when to breathe. This comes from early reading teaching where children are often told to 'take a little breath' when they see a full stop. In fact, of course, we often do breathe at the end of a sentence when we read aloud because that's when it's least disruptive to the meaning. However, punctuation is not linked to respiration; it's linked to meaning.

Thinking points

- Teachers generally associate teaching punctuation with teaching writing, but it's as important to talk about punctuation when teaching reading. The punctuation controls the meaning of a text, and varying the punctuation can change the meaning of a sentence entirely. The title of the bestselling book *Eats, Shoots & Leaves* by Lynn Truss (Profile Books, 2003) shows how adding a comma can make a prosaic description of a panda's diet (eats shoots and leaves) into something altogether more dramatic.

- In order for children to engage fully with what they read, they need to understand how the words are linked together: which work together in a phrase or clause, which combine to form a sentence, why a writer has joined two sentences to make a compound or complex sentence. Without recognising the punctuation, children won't know how to read with expression.

Tips, ideas and activities

- Ask children to listen to you reading another language or sentences made up of strings of nonsense syllables. How can they tell when you have finished a sentence? Ask them to listen to your voice as it rises and falls.

- Try speaking to children in a robotic, deadpan voice. Discuss how much more difficult it is to make meaning of what you say if your voice isn't adding colour to your words with rising and falling intonation, and expression. Explain that reading without paying attention to intonation is like speaking in that robotic way and that it is the punctuation in a piece of writing that gives clues as to how it should be read.

- Have discussions around the idea of a sentence with your children. What do they know about sentences? Collect their information and agree a class definition. (For example: 'A sentence begins with a capital letter, ends with punctuation and makes sense by itself'.) As you do shared reading, compare sentences from the text against the class definition. Does the definition hold up, or does it need to be tweaked?

- Teach children 'kung-fu punctuation', to draw their attention to punctuation marks in their reading. In this system, children have to make a particular kung-fu move when they see different punctuation marks. You might want to try varying the kung-fu moves, using noises or movements. Any of these mechanisms will draw children's attention to punctuation.

- Talk about question marks and exclamation marks as being in the same family as full stops – they can all occur at the end of sentences. Explore what happens when you read the same words with different punctuation marks: *You're right. You're right? You're right!*

- Use activities like these to help children to recognise that punctuation marks are there to help them to make their reading make sense.

You Can... **Enliven your reading aloud**

Do you have children in your class who are over-reliant on phonics and who sound out every word on every line, no matter how common the word? Or are there children who read in a flat, quiet monotone, mumbling over so many words it's impossible to know whether they are reading the words or not? If this isn't yet a reading difficulty it's about to become one, so it's worth taking immediate action.

Thinking points

● Teaching children to read by hearing them read aloud is an unnatural thing to do: people very rarely have to read aloud once they have stopped 'learning to read', unless they are teachers or parents. In asking children to read aloud, you are demanding that they perform two tasks simultaneously: the first is to decode at word and sentence level and make meaning (which is what we all do when we read to ourselves); the second is to make meaning by using intonation and expression at text level. Unlike reading at word and sentence level, where all the clues that children need are visible in the word, reading at text level means that they have to be able to use their knowledge of language structures and intonation.

Tips, ideas and activities

● Check children's instant recognition of high-frequency words (see page 9 and the synthetic phonics scheme, *Letters and Sounds* (DfES, 2007) for more information). Do they have to work these words out or can they say them immediately?

● Have hearing and vision checked: if a child is struggling against the odds, then reading is likely to be flat and uninteresting.

● Read playscripts together, with a group of patient children and your target child. (Choose a playscript that allows for quick turn-taking.) The target child will be able to build up an understanding of the plot by listening to the other children read. Also, playscripts are intended to be read aloud, so it's often easier to understand the feelings being expressed by the speaker and expression therefore comes more naturally.

● Use a tape recorder. Tape yourself and the child reading together. Ask the child to discuss differences between their reading aloud and yours. Can they *hear* differences?

● Read the same passage aloud yourself – once in a flat monotone and once with expression. Can the child recognise any differences between the two readings?

● Give the child the opportunity to read at least some of a text quietly to themselves, before you ask them to read aloud. Does developing some familiarity with the text help at all? If so, tape-record it so that the child has a model of their own voice against which to compare future performances.

● Let the child reread some familiar and easier books and invite them to play games while they read. Ask them to read very slowly, as fast as they can, in a high- or low-pitched voice, with lots of expression or with no expression at all.

● Pair the child with a reader from a younger class who is even less confident, and explain that the younger child needs help. Their help should include modelling reading aloud.

You Can... **Make your teaching dyslexia friendly**

If ten per cent of the British population are dyslexic, the chances are high that you will have dyslexic learners in your class. Only the severely affected three or four per cent of learners will need specific dyslexia interventions, but all children who struggle with reading will benefit if you adapt your teaching to make it dyslexia friendly.

Thinking points

● At the moment, definitions of dyslexia vary. Research in the neurological sciences is fast catching up with finding physiological and neurological ways of diagnosing dyslexia, but for now we need to continue to look out for children whose: vocabulary and general knowledge is much better than their performance in literacy; processing short-term memory is very poor (for example children who can't remember a series of instructions); ability to remember and to manipulate phonemes is limited; organisational and sequencing skills are inadequate.

● Dyslexic children are more likely to be boys, but the proportion of girls is still high enough for concern. If you have worries about any children in your class, ask your SENCO to arrange a proper dyslexia screen. However, both before and after the dyslexia screen, children will continue to present with the same problems so modifying your teaching style may well support them.

Tips, ideas and activities

● Use photocopiable page 58 as a brief checklist of difficulties often faced by children with dyslexia.

● Pace it. Dyslexic children learn best if the important information is fed to them in small bursts and is revisited frequently. Instead of one long lesson, can you break it up into three smaller chunks, each with the same learning objective, which will give opportunities for a change of pace and activity? This is especially important in lessons like literacy, science and humanities where children have to take in so much information aurally.

● Activate VAKT. Dyslexic children will have their preferred learning style (which is less likely to be auditory) and ideally they will need multi-sensory learning opportunities which allow all four routes to learning to be active at the same time. Use pictures as often as possible, but be aware that many dyslexic children find it difficult to multitask, so if they are studying a picture they may not be able to take in what you are saying at the same time.

● Think laterally. If one way of teaching something doesn't work, can you find another way? Repeating important objectives in a different way is more likely to help to reinforce them, but it will also give children who didn't 'get it' the first time the opportunity to try again.

● Know your children. Dyslexic children have to concentrate so much harder than the rest, that their concentration spans tend to be shorter and they get tired more quickly. Learn to recognise the signs so that you know when children can't take in any more until they have had a short brain break.

● Be patient. Like everyone, dyslexic children have good and bad days. But their bad days can be so much worse than everyone else's. If you are frustrated by how quickly a child forgets something or by the fact that they are disorganised, think of how they must feel. Dyslexic children are not disorganised on purpose – they just aren't wired for sequential, organised activities.

You Can... **Read puzzle books**

Puzzle books are an ideal way to encourage children to read: they are generally seen to be 'cool', they are easy to find and appropriate for a variety of ages and the texts tend to be comparatively short. Most importantly, however, the reading has an immediate and direct purpose – if children don't read the text, then they don't know how to solve the puzzle.

Thinking points

● One difficulty with motivating reluctant readers is that very often they don't see the purpose of reading. If they live in a visual and audio dominated environment, then their experience of reading may be that it is generally accompanied by visual or audio support from which they can derive more information.

● Puzzle books can provide a satisfying half-way house between the books where all of the information is in the text and those where the pictures play a significant part in the comprehension: in these books the answer may be in the picture but the question is always in the text. Once reluctant readers have been introduced to puzzle books, many find that the challenge of solving the puzzle makes the challenge of 'solving' the text worthwhile.

Tips, ideas and activities

● Puzzle books and puzzle texts come in a wide variety of shapes and sizes. Many of them are not necessarily books that you would choose for your children, since they are rarely 'great literature', but if they get children reading and engaging with texts, they can be a useful stepping stone.

● Some of the easier books to read, and often the most intriguing for the reluctant reader, are books where the puzzle is entirely visual. The *Where's Wally?* books (Walker Books) have been around for years but most children will willingly pore over pictures searching for that red and white striped hat. Although it is inconspicuous on the page, there is always some text which both contextualises the puzzle in terms of what else is happening in the 'story' and also sets additional challenges. The success of these books has spawned a variety of other puzzle books which have a short text that directs you to search for something in the pictures.

● Other puzzle books have more of a story, so require more reading in order to understand what is going on, but still the focus is on finding details in pictures to find the clues that will be needed for the next step of the story.

● There are also more literary puzzle books, where the puzzles may take the form of riddles. Here the answer is often in a picture, but first the reader has to have read and appreciated a play on words before they know what to look for in pictures. Well-constructed riddle books are often very popular with reluctant readers who glow with pleasure when they manage to work out how the words have been used to create the puzzle.

You Can... **Read art**

By the time they are in Key Stage 2, most children have spent years reading pictures in early reading books as well as those in cartoon series on TV. You can utilise and develop this expertise in order to teach comprehension skills away from the page. Children who refuse to open a book of words are much more likely to respond more positively to books of artistic images.

Thinking points

● Teaching comprehension is more than just a hoop that you need children to jump through when they are 10 or 11. Comprehension is a life skill that extends beyond the page and into children's lives: they need to be able to understand what people are saying to them both at the literal and at the inferential level; they need to be able to understand what's going on both in films and in conversations around them; they need to learn to make sense of their world.

● Using art as the basis for teaching comprehension is very inclusive and has equal value for your reluctant readers and your more enthusiastic readers. You can develop key literacy skills through speaking and listening, using visual images only.

Tips, ideas and activities

● Teach comprehension through art routinely, across the curriculum. Through an internet connection and an interactive whiteboard, you have access to the collections of the world's finest museums, as well as to enormous collections of visuals in commercial illustration and photograph collections. Make use of this facility across the curriculum as you find visual images that are relevant to your topics.

● Teach children to distinguish between various different types of comprehension questions while you are looking at a picture. Focus on:
  ● What the picture shows (Reading Assessment Focus 2 (AF2)) *What colour is the...?; What can you see on the...?*
  ● What can be inferred or deduced (AF3) *Why do you think the...? What do you think has just happened/is about to happen? What do you think this person is thinking?*
  ● The structure of the work, examining choices the artist made (AF4) *Why might the painter have put this here and not over there? Why do you think this is a sculpture, not a canvas?*
  ● The intentions of the artist and the impact on the audience (AF6) *Do you like this image? What do you think the artist is trying to communicate?*
  ● The historical and cultural origins of the work (AF7) *How can you tell that this was painted during a particular time or event? Look at these pictures from another culture. How have they influenced this artist?*

● Use art with the whole class working together around the whiteboards, or as groups working around smaller pictures. All children will benefit from the experience of articulating their responses to the different types of question.

● Use the art as the basis for drama techniques such as freeze-frame and hot-seating. In this way, children's responses and understanding of the different kinds of comprehension question can be developed.

You Can... **Read comics**

After years of being considered to be somehow a waste of time, comics are now beginning to creep into schools. In many classrooms they are still consigned to the wet playtime baskets, but at least they are no longer being confiscated and thrown into the bin. As so many children seem to enjoy them and feel motivated to read them, let's start welcoming the comic as another genre.

Thinking points

● Although they are not generally recognised as good quality literature, comics have been motivating children to read for generations. They have a number of attributes which make them appealing to the reluctant reader: they are not too demanding; the pictures reinforce the important words; the stories are usually uncomplicated; they are often about characters and events which are familiar from the TV.

● If you are asking children to accept your choice of books without complaint, you should be equally as accepting of theirs. If there are comic-reading reluctant readers in the class, welcome their comics as part of your teaching and recognise them as a valid resource for reading.

Tips, ideas and activities

● Most of the genres you teach in your literacy sessions will have a counterpart in comics: comics have stories set in familiar settings, which are often funny; there are fantasy stories galore as well as adventure and suspense stories and there are stories set in the past as well as those in the future.

● When you are teaching a literary skill – for example, how settings are critical to events or how writers create suspense – explore these both through comics and other books you are reading. Many children, in addition to your reluctant readers, will benefit from access to the comics since they can use the visuals to support the words. In creating characters, the comic artist has to make the same kinds of decisions as an author, except that the comic artist has got two media through which to portray the character (words and illustrations) whereas the writer has only got words (except in the case of picture books).

● Allow reluctant readers to use a comic story as the basis of written work they do for you. Encourage them to pore over the story and find the same kinds of evidence that other children are finding in the fully written text.

● Include comics in your class library and give them the same status as books. It will be important to their readers that they are recognised as appropriate reading material.

● Accept the fact that all children in your class may never get lost in a book of your choice. As their teacher, it is important that you widen children's horizons and introduce them to books, authors and poets who you admire. However, at the same time, you may need to be prepared to let them widen your horizons and introduce you to a book genre that they admire. It is important to them that you are seen to respect what's important to them. If comics are part of their culture, be pleased that they are at least reading.

You Can... **Read magazines and newspapers**

If a child in your class has an interest or a hobby, there might be a specialist magazine available to support their interest. If it's an interest which is shared by many youngsters, you are likely to find age-appropriate magazines, sticker-books and so on. You can make use of these non-fiction texts in your teaching.

Thinking points

● Magazines and newspapers are of interest to a wide range of children. Even children who can't yet read, or who won't read, will often be drawn to the pictures and captions if the magazine matches their interests.

● Newspapers are also popular among some children who may read them alongside their parents. On the whole, the 'red tops' are more likely to appeal to children of this age, especially if these include 'inside information' and pictures of their favourite celebrities. Children often watch the news, even if reluctantly, while waiting for their chosen programmes to come on, and are often aware of the main news stories. This prior knowledge can be invaluable for them when they are reading today's developments in a story.

Tips, ideas and activities

● Welcoming magazines or sticker-books may be something of an innovation in school. If so, you might want to set some boundaries about sticker trading. Why not hold a weekly, supervised session in which stickers can be traded legitimately, then returned to an envelope and a teacher for the rest of the day?

● Sticker-books and magazines tend to have short, informative pieces about football players, fish, cleaning a pony's tack or whatever the theme is. Use these model texts as part of your literacy work relating to reports, explanatory or instructional texts. Look, with children, at how information is dispersed between captions, statistics and main texts. Talk about where to start reading on a page and how to synthesise the information. Many of your reluctant readers may turn out to be experts at using information from a variety of sources to gain a fuller picture.

● Make use of any child's reading of a newspaper – be it national, local or community. Talk to individual children about *how* they read newspapers and about *what* they gain from the experience. Again, you may find that children are managing to gather information from the TV or radio news and they are adding to that news by reading stories in the paper.

● Newspapers are also the ideal starting point for class discussions and debates, leading to a more developed understanding of persuasive and discursive texts. Carefully selected articles from the 'red tops' are more likely to fuel a debate and to provide samples of biased and persuasive reporting.

● It is too easy to assume that because children don't choose to read the texts you provide them with in school, that they are reluctant to engage with any texts. Give opportunities for children to show you and their classmates what they can do when they are allowed to choose their reading matter: you may be surprised.

You Can... **Read TV and film**

Most children can read a screen very effectively, without being aware of what they are doing. It would be useful to be able to harness this expertise in reading on-screen to create a willingness to read a book. But first, you should celebrate children's existing competencies and develop their comprehension skills.

Thinking points

● The National Schools Film Week (www.nsfw.org) happens each year in October/November. Although the majority of films are for secondary children, there is always at least one widely available film open for primary children. Films are screened all over the country and the only cost to schools is the cost of the coach: the viewing is completely free (but book early as the best films fill-up fast). For some children, it may be their first experience of going to the cinema, and ideas are available from www.filmeducation.org for making the most of the experience.

● Taking your class to a cinema is a very unifying experience which can be built on back in school both in terms of a shared event and in terms of working on projects related to the film.

Tips, ideas and activities

● Questions that require children's understanding of the craft of an author can be addressed through film and TV. Multimodal literacies (using more than one medium for teaching and learning) are embedded in the curriculum now, so it is becoming easier to find suitable resources.

● Most TV channels now have websites where programmes are made available to watch after they have been screened. See, for example, www.bbc.co.uk/iplayer or www.channel4.com/4od/index.html

● The interactive whiteboard now allows you to offer a 'cinema experience' in your classroom. Take advantage of it to watch extracts from appropriate programmes and films. Then, when you want to discuss how suspense is built in a novel, you can begin by considering how suspense is built in the BBC's *Dr Who* for example: the same questions are asked by producers and directors as those that you and your children puzzle over in the classroom. Once children are aware of the way in which atmosphere is developed on-screen, they will be more receptive to considering how it is dealt with in a book.

● If you can access a film and a book of the same story (such as the *Harry Potter* series (Warner Bros. (films)/Bloomsbury (books)) compare the way in which parts of the story are handled in the different media. *Willy Wonker & the Chocolate Factory* (David L. Wopler Productions,1971) and *Charlie and the Chocolate factory* (Warner Bros.,2005) can be compared with each other and with the Roald Dahl book.)

● Children's TV programmes will also include dramas based on favourite books. There are also often links between comics and cartoon series on TV. It is generally acknowledged that children can learn techniques of literary analysis through a diverse collection of media.

SUNNYVILLE PRIMARY
Film screening - 1pm

You Can... **Read computer games**

Computer games are often linked with violence and with lack of sleep and there is little doubt that many of the games played by your children are not aimed at their age group. However, that is not a good reason to dismiss all computer games from your consideration: many games involve ongoing reading and many children will persevere to read these texts which matter to them.

Thinking points

● Commercial computer games are increasingly being played in schools. This revolution started in the secondary sector and is becoming increasingly common in Key Stage 2 classrooms. In 2006, a MORI poll showed that over 90% of Key Stage 2 teachers recognised that many computer games have an educational value; at the same time 59% of teachers said that they would be happy to use computer games in the classroom.

● The games which are generally more popular in primary classrooms are simulation games like *Zoo Tycoon*® and *The Sims*™. In these games, children have to use strategic thinking to decide how to develop the simulation, weighing up different factors. These games are valued because they generate speaking and listening and encourage the use of literacy skills.

Tips, ideas and activities

● Ask children to bring in their games from home. Set limits as to the kind of game you are willing to host in the classroom – try insisting that the age guidance on the packaging is adhered to.

● Invite children to make a short presentation to the class, explaining how the game works, what its key strengths are, how much language is used in the game and so on.

● Set up children as groups of 'games reviewers': each group should evaluate the games they are looking at and decide which are the most useful for your teaching in the classroom. Share the focus you have decided on: you may want to look at games which encourage reading, or those which develop speaking and listening, thinking and decision-making skills, strategic thinking, working co-operatively.

● Give opportunities for children to play the games – and to demonstrate their prowess on their game. This doesn't have to be a sustained gaming session but ten minutes twice a week will allow a variety of children to show what they can do.

● Focus on games which require a lot of reading. Ask your reluctant readers what it is about the screen text that makes it worth the challenge of struggling to read it. Who helps them at home? How much effort will they put in? What's the reward? Can you use the results of these conversations to put in place some kind of reward system where children will make the same amount of effort when reading for you if you allow them to play with their games occasionally?

You Can... **Read from the internet**

How often have you had a child who has printed off an entire entry from an on-line encyclopaedia as evidence that they are interested in a current topic? On the one hand, these efforts are to be congratulated, because an effort has been made, but on the other hand if the child hasn't read any of what has been printed off, then it has little value. But you can encourage reluctant readers to use the internet and improve their reading.

Thinking points

● Does your school have a learning platform, such as a Managed Learning Environment (MLE) or a Virtual Learning Environment (VLE)? Do many of your children have access to the internet from home? How do you encourage responsible internet use away from school premises? Do you have a list of internet sites which you feel are appropriate for your class to explore from home?

● It may be worth your while investing some time to find out about how your children use the internet either at home or using community facilities. Does the school or local authority have guidance which will help to keep them safe? And if so, have you taught it to your children? Spending dedicated ICT time giving children the tools they need to keep safe on the internet is as worthwhile as giving them the skills to stay safe in water during PE lessons.

Tips, ideas and activities

● As well as teaching children how to use search engines, why not teach them how to search particular websites which are dedicated to schools' learning? For example, www.bbc.co.uk/schools offers a wide range of activities and information on most of the topics you will study in school. Other sites like www.educationcity.co.uk or www.atschool.co.uk have curriculum-based activities aimed specifically at Key Stage 2 children. In addition, these websites include carefully selected links to other appropriate and researched websites that your children might enjoy.

● Teach children how to read the websites: show them where to start reading, talk about what needs to be read carefully and what can be skimmed. Explain that they don't have to read everything on the page but headings and links should be scanned to help them to navigate to the most relevant sections of the site, which can then be read in detail.

● Ensure that all children are aware that if they are asked to do a piece of original writing, the internet is a useful starting point for research, but the text should never be simply copied, pasted and presented as their own work.

● Teach children how to edit e-text for summarising or fact-finding exercises, using the on-screen highlighter pens and different colours for the text. Your reluctant readers may be willing to participate in this process, since it allows them to acknowledge that some texts are 'too hard' and to develop strategies for reading and getting the most from the texts. Many children will find it much easier to learn these skills working from e-texts than working from paper texts.

● Teaching the use of on-screen tools that can be used for editing is often a more successful approach to teaching comprehension than just using the well-established methods of skimming and scanning. Text marking, pasting and cutting may be much more motivating approaches for reluctant readers.

You Can... Sequence ideas and events in a non-fiction text

Sometimes children are reluctant to read because they derive little pleasure from the process of decoding text without managing to make meaning. Teaching children strategies for identifying and sequencing ideas and events in non-fiction texts can build a powerful tool for them to use to make the most of a text.

Thinking points

● Teachers are often better at presenting opportunities for children to practise reading comprehension than they are at actually teaching strategies for making meaning. Reading comprehension is such a tricky area of reading because it means different things to different people. The comprehension strategies recommended with the simple view of reading (prediction, visualization, questioning, sequencing, summarizing, clarifying) envisage that children will explore their response to a text in a wide variety of different modes, whereas the QCA Assessment Focuses (i: decoding, ii: finding evidence in a text, iii: inference and deduction, iv: text structure, v: author's language, vi: purpose and impact of a text, vii: cultural and historical contexts) are perhaps more suited to written comprehension activities. What do you think reading comprehension should be about?

Tips, ideas and activities

● It is often easier to teach comprehension skills using non-fiction texts because the passages that children have to read and make sense of are so much more compact. What's more, the topic sentences are a good way of getting the gist of what a paragraph will be about.

● Teach children a systematic approach to reading non-fiction:
  ○ They should first try to create a mental map of the passage of pages. What are the main and sub-headings? Where are the illustrations and captions? Are there diagrams, maps or tables?
  ○ Teach them to use topic sentences to predict what each paragraph is about. In well written non-fiction books the topic sentence, or first sentence, introduces and sometimes summarises the information to be given in the paragraph. They should skim read the passage, focusing mainly on the topic sentences each time.
  ○ They should then reread the text paragraph by paragraph. As they finish each paragraph, they should try to think about what it was about. If they don't understand, they should reread it. Teach them not to continue to read if they can't make sense of a paragraph (unless they're in an exam setting).

● Show them different diagrams on which they can record the ideas and events they read about. Include opportunities for them to jot down their own questions. The National Curriculum non-fiction fliers (www.standards.dfes.gov.uk/ primary/casestudies/literacy) include useful 'skeletons' for recording ideas found in different types of text. These are the same as the skeletons for writing, you just use them for recording ideas from a text instead.

You Can... **Find the main idea**

One of the challenges that faces many children when they read is that they have to decode a lot of words, each of which has a number of potential meanings, and they have to think about what the point of each sentence, paragraph or passage is. You can support children in making more sense of their reading by helping them to find the main idea.

Thinking points

● Articulating the main idea in a passage is an art form. There are two challenges: first the reader has to decide which of many potential ideas is the main one, and second they have to try to articulate it in their own words. There is often some overlap between inarticulate children and reluctant readers and for these children rephrasing something can present its own challenge. Often the rephrasing is longer and more complicated than the original!

● Before you begin to teach children to state the main idea, try it yourself and think about the strategies and skills you call upon. If you have experienced the thought-processes yourself, you will probably be able to explain it to children more successfully.

Tips, ideas and activities

● Before you ask children to state the main idea of a piece of text, let them practise using pictures. Show them pictures – perhaps illustrations from unfamiliar books – and ask children to explain what each one is about: an illustration will show lots of enriching details but it will essentially be about one main idea. The main idea could be establishing an atmosphere, giving information about a character, showing an event in a story, explaining a process, giving information about an event and so on. Use this activity to establish the difference between important and useful details and the main idea.

● Introduce 'the main idea' in a simple text. Select your paragraph carefully to begin with: the main idea in a story might be the next event, creating a setting or explaining the relationship between two characters. In a non-fiction text, it might be setting the scene, explaining a step in a process or describing one part of something in a report text.

● When they tell you the main idea ask the child to focus on a two-part answer: the first part should tell you what the function of the paragraph is and the second should let you know what it contains.

● Finding the main idea is very challenging for many children. But in the same way that you can't appreciate a picture until you know what it portrays, you can't fully understand a text until you can tell what it is about.

● Try matching the main idea in a picture with its corresponding text. For some children, directly applying the ideas from the pictures can support them in finding key ideas in the text.

You Can... **Summarise**

Summarising is a key skill in reading – as it is in speaking and listening. If a child can summarise the content of a text, ideally using fewer words than the author did in the original, you can be confident that they have engaged with and understood the text. But until you have taught them how to summarise, they are unlikely to do it successfully.

Thinking points

● Listen to news and current affairs programmes on the TV and radio, particularly those where the interviewer has an aggressive style. You will constantly hear them trying to summarise the view expressed by the interviewee and instead end up confusing the audience. What's more, although summarising should take up fewer words than the original, even seasoned interviewers can end up using more words than their interviewees!

● Your children have the advantage that they don't have to do their summaries orally, but nonetheless they will benefit from time and opportunities to practise. Reluctant readers need to know for themselves whether or not they have understood what they have read, and checking that they can summarise the text is a useful way of finding out.

Tips, ideas and activities

● Summarising is quite an abstract skill, so you will probably want to present children with multiple-choice questions first. Phrasing a question along the following lines can be very supportive: *Which of these sentences is the best summary of the events in chapter 5?; of the views expressed by Miss X?; of the process of pasteurising milk?* You can then teach children the process which is:

  ● To carefully read each of the options, marking the key words and ideas.
  ● To reread the text, marking key words and ideas.
  ● To reread each of the options, evaluating them in the light of the text.
  ● To select the one which best expresses the same view as the text.

● Giving children the opportunity to select from a number of choices removes the need to consider how to rephrase the information. If you find it difficult to summarise the ideas in a text, the text you have selected may be too difficult, or inappropriate, for children to use for this purpose.

● Once you have given children opportunities to explore possible summaries, begin to ask them to summarise the ideas themselves. In the early stages, they will benefit from opportunities to mark a text. A process for doing this is:

  ● Highlighting the key words and ideas within each sentence in a short paragraph or text (between three and five lines).
  ● Crossing out any additional details.
  ● Trying to rephrase the key ideas, shortening them from four or five sentences to one or two sentences.

● Continue to give opportunities to select from the best summaries of texts. In this way, children will experience reading well-constructed sentences containing key information only.

● Encourage children to read and write blurbs for books as one way of summarising a lot of information into a very short space.

You Can... Predict what will happen next

Teaching children how to think forwards and to recognise the impact of cause and effect is a key skill for reading. Predicting should begin from the moment a child picks up a book to read it. If you can teach them to activate prior knowledge by looking at everything from the size of the print, to the cover images, to the writing on the covers, you will increase their chances of succeeding when they read a book.

Thinking points

● Considering the implications of an action is a life skill as well as a reading skill. Unfortunately, it's a skill that some of your reluctant readers may find difficult in every context so if you can teach them to think ahead in reading, they may learn a useful, transferable skill.

● Prediction is a skill which needs to be addressed at the appropriate level and through the appropriate channel for each individual child. If you feel that some of these ideas are too easy or too challenging for some pupils, adapt the activities to make them work.

Tips, ideas and activities

● Teaching predicting through a variety of multi-sensory activities will make it fun. Once children have acquired the basic idea, it's easier to transfer to reading, partly because you will have agreed a language to talk about what you're doing.

● Watch DVDs/videos of slapstick comedy or cartoons like *Road Runner*. Pause the programme at a comedy moment and ask children both what is likely to happen next and how they know. Help them to articulate the strategies they are using to work out what will happen next.

● Introduce children to the topology of a book. Help them to make predictions from the moment they hear the title: how can they use the title, or the author's name, or the cover illustrations, the blurb or a quick flick through the book to predict the contents? Teaching children to activate their prior knowledge and expectations will give them a head start.

● Read stories to children and stop to discuss what might happen next. Again, once you have enjoyed the discussion, talk about strategies used. Help them to recognise that prediction uses information from many different places, for example:
  ○ Information from the text.
  ○ Information from knowledge of the types of events that occur in stories.
  ○ Information gathered about stereotypical characters or settings.
  ○ Information from their knowledge of society and culture
  ○ General knowledge.

You Can... **Explore what's *not* been said**

There has been some confusion about whether or not inference and deduction are the same thing. Now we agree that they're not. Deduction involves using clues and information which have been given in the text to work out – or deduce – what's going on in a story; inference involves using an understanding of life, society and stories in order to assume information that the writer hasn't explicitly given.

Thinking points

● Inference and deduction are often referred to as higher-order reading skills because they involve reading between the lines. However, children are constantly inferring and deducing all through the day. When you wish the class *Good morning*, children infer that you want them to be quiet and listen; when they see a set of spelling books on a table top, they deduce that a spelling lesson is imminent. Inference and deduction are skills which most children use throughout the day both at home and at school.

● Grab children's attention by teaching inference and deduction from the standpoint of a detective. The role of a detective is to deduce *what* might have happened by using the clues around and then to infer *why* it might have happened using their own experience and worldly knowledge.

Tips, ideas and activities

● Give children notebooks in which they can rule two columns: *what* and *why*. In a variety of contexts, let them use their notebooks to make notes, recording their experience of using inference and deduction.

● Give each group of children a bag of shopping. This can either be a real bag of items, a shopping list made up from pictures from on-line catalogues or simply a list of items.

　○ Ask children to write down what they can deduce about the people whose shopping it is (*Is it a family? Is there a baby? Is it a child's shopping list?*) and then ask them to infer why the list might have been compiled (*Weekly shop? Shopping for the birth of a baby? Birthday present list?*)

　○ Talk about how children worked out the answers using their clues. Let groups who had the same shopping bags share notes. Did they all make the same inferences and deductions? Share differences.

　○ Let children make up shopping lists for each other from which to make inferences and deductions.

● Find photographs of people on the internet. Make lists about what you can infer and deduce from the images. Children of this age are generally beginning to develop stereotypical ideas about people. Although stereotypes have their dangers, they are often useful starting points for developing understanding so encourage discussion – and make use of anti-stereotypical images too.

● Once children have practised their skills using objects or pictures, give them texts and different coloured highlighter pens. Ask a question that involves either inference or deduction and have children to use an appropriate highlighter to highlight the words and phrases which they used to work out the answer.

You Can... Read poetry together

Developing a shared passion for poetry is one of the most worthwhile experiences for a teacher to share with a class. Different classes enjoy different kinds of poetry and finding out what your class likes can be one of the exciting explorations of the autumn term. In many classrooms, poetry is under-represented in teaching, in reading aloud to the class and in children's choice of reading.

Thinking points

● Poems are often an ideal way in to reading for reluctant readers. Poems have so much going for them: they are often short so don't require too much sustained concentration; they can be funny or memorable; the rhythm and rhyme can provide significant clues about words both on the first and subsequent readings.

● One of the strongest reasons for encouraging your reluctant readers to engage with poetry is that it can bolster their image of themselves as readers. Reluctant readers often find themselves being presented with shorter, easier texts than their peers. With a poem, it's much harder to determine whether it's easier, and a short poem is just a short poem – it hasn't been written that way to make it easier to read. (You may have chosen it for its readability, but that's another story.)

Tips, ideas and activities

● Introduce children to more accessible poems first. There are a number of anthologies around that focus on nonsense poems or funny poems. These often appeal to the reluctant reader because the poems are short, humorous and have a regular rhyme and rhythm.

● Use websites like www.gigglepoetry.com and allow children to browse through a variety of different styles of accessible funny poems in order to develop their own choices and opinions.

● Go to www.poetryarchive.org or a similar website to hear poets reading aloud from their own poems. Talk about how they use their voice to make the poem sound interesting.

● Create regular one-minute poetry slots during your school day where you or one of the children reads a poem you have enjoyed. Try to emulate poets you hear on-line in using your voice to add expression and aid meaning.

● Invite a poet into school to perform and read from their own poems. If possible, ask the poet to conduct a reciting workshop either with your whole class or just with your reluctant readers. The experience of reciting and performing a poem can be very motivating.

● Choose poems you enjoy as a class and have a go at writing your versions of them. Polish them and then publish them on the web. Try sites like www.poetryclass.net/kids.htm, www.maninthemoon.co.uk or www.poetryzone.ndirect.co.uk; send them your class poem, or the best of your children's poems. Send a letter home with the web address and suggest to children that as well as showing their family their poem, they should read it aloud.

You Can... **Play with rhyme**

Developing an awareness of rhyme is vital for both reading and writing. In reading, it helps children to develop sensitivity for visual spelling patterns so that they can recognise words which share spelling patterns and therefore which might sound the same. In writing, it supports spelling by analogy. In both reading and writing, it helps to strengthen children's awareness of the sounds and patterns of language.

Thinking points

● Rhyming activities are generally very popular with children. As a teacher, it's important to be aware of unintended and inappropriate rhymes – but for children that's often part of the fun. Children often associate rhyme with language that happens outside of the classroom, for example playground rhymes, football chants and pop songs. For this reason, rhyme has a more liberated feel than some other aspects of literacy teaching. You can exploit this sense of fun in your teaching.

● Developing children's awareness of the way that rhyme is used in poetry and songs can help them to understand why the grammar or word choice in some lines may seem very awkward, but at the same time it sensitises them to the power of rhyming words in holding the interest of the listener.

Tips, ideas and activities

● Play with simple rhyming poems together, such as those by Spike Milligan or Edward Lear. Explore what happens when you alter the last word in a line of a poem. What is the impact on the rest of the poem?

● Read rhyming riddles together. Talk about the structure of the riddle in giving clues but not telling the whole story. Explore why it's easier to solve a riddle in rhyme than not in rhyme.

● Ask children to bring in lyrics from suitable pop songs or download them from the web (copyright permitting). Allow children to use highlighters to identify rhymes.

● Teach them to describe rhyming patterns in the grown-up way of allocating a letter to each rhyme (for example, the rhyming pattern of 'Jack and Jill' is *aabccb* whereas 'Humpty Dumpty' is *aabb*).

● Give children simple poems to read (see lists of websites on page 27) where you have blanked out some rhyming words. Ask children to predict what the missing word is each time. Discuss how they decided on each word.

● Cut up poems so that children need to recognise pairs of rhyming words in order to rebuild the poem correctly. Once they have completed the 'poem jigsaw' let them share their ideas with others and compare answers.

● Give children opportunities to write little rhymes. It's much harder than it looks and it will give children the chance to find out more about how rhymes work. Teach them how to use a rhyming dictionary to help them in their task.

● Give children experiences of listening to poems read aloud where the rhyme is very prominent, and to comparing the same poem to one where the rhyme is used more subtly. Ask children to compare the experience as a listener. Which poem did they prefer listening to?

You Can... **Recognise rhythm and beat**

Developing an awareness of rhythm and beat is not only great fun, but also very useful for reading longer words as understanding rhythm helps children to explore pronunciation of words of more than one syllable. Many of the more accessible poetry forms have very strong rhythms which can help children in predicting language – which is very supportive of the more hesitant reader.

Thinking points

● Rhythm and beat are fundamental features of any language, so developing an understanding of how rhythm functions within a language is key for reading effectively and successfully. Children need to recognise the distinction between rhythm and beat. The 'beat' is a steady, regular pulse, whereas the 'rhythm' is based on the number of syllables. Consider the four steady beats in each line of:

Jack and **Jill** went **up** the **hill** to **fetch** a **pail** of **wat-er**.

There are the same four beats in each line, but the rhythm of each line is quite distinct.

Tips, ideas and activities

● Use music lessons to explore setting familiar rhymes to music using both a steady beat and a rhythm. You can either have children using body percussion or using different instruments. If you have a child in your class who is a keyboard player, they may be able to demonstrate setting the keyboard to play the beat while they tap out the tune in rhythm.

● As you read and reread rhymes with strong rhythms and beats, give children practice so that they can recognise the beat and the rhythm easily. This will help them to read new poems more accurately, but understanding how the beat and rhythm interrelate will give them a better understanding about why poets sometimes order words in unusual ways so that they can keep to the rhythm and rhyme pattern. Introduce the technical term 'scansion'.

● Talk about the places where the rhythm and the beat coincide. On which syllable do they both generally occur? (It's usually the first.) Begin to compile a group list of words where the beat and rhythm coincide on the second or third syllable. Explore the first syllables of these words (for example, a**cross**, im**poss**ible, un**like**ly). Help children to recognise that these first, unstressed, syllables are often prefixes.

● Introduce the idea of stressed and unstressed syllables. Discuss how the meaning changes when you change the stress of the syllables in im**poss**ible to **im**possible.

● Share some poems which don't have a strong, regular beat. Do the lines still have rhythm? Compare, for example, the rhythms of natural speech in many of Michael Rosen's poems with the steady beat of many of Roger McGough's poems.

● Teach children some limericks. Once they are familiar, the constraint of rhythm and rhyme in these poems make them very predictable and satisfying to read.

You Can... **Read line by line**

Once children have some awareness and understanding of the patterns of rhythm and rhyme, you can encourage them to read by making poems into puzzles for them to enjoy. Sharing poems little by little in this way can excite many children into wanting to have a satisfactory ending, so they will read on to find it. This can also encourage reluctant readers to read more.

Thinking points

● Do you have a poetry section in your school or class library? Is it well used? If not, you could try setting up trails of lines from parts of poems which lead children to the poetry section. Hang individual lines of a poem from the ceiling, make a trail along a corridor, or make giant footsteps each with an individual line from a poem. You could leave the poem incomplete and let children find the endings for themselves. Different Key Stage 2 classes could take turns in making a poetry trail for the rest of the school to enjoy. In this way, all of the children in your class can participate in making their own stage of the trail, copying out their line and providing an illustration or border. If you laminate the trails, you can keep them and reuse them next year.

Tips, ideas and activities

● Provide poems with missing words, these may well be rhyming words or words with a particular rhythm. Give children a choice of words they could use to fill each space and ask them to share their strategies for deciding which words to use each time.

● Photocopy a poem (copyright permitting) and ask children to cut it up into a given number of pieces to make a poem jigsaw for other children to complete. Discuss ways of cutting the poem up: it could be into verses, into pairs of lines, into sets of three lines so that rhyme can be used to solve the puzzle. Alternatively, verses can be cut vertically so that half of two lines is on one jigsaw piece and the other half of the lines is on the other. Before the children cut up their poems, discuss strategies they will need to use to solve the poem puzzles and then ask them to cut the poems to enable those strategies to be used.

● Present children with a number of limericks, each with their final line missing. Discuss with the children what the final line might be in each case. You can either provide the final lines, or ask children to write their own, taking into account the rhythm and rhyme.

● Write out a poem using a different colour for each verse. Cut the poem into individual lines and mix them up. Give each child in the class or group one of the lines and ask them to get themselves in order so that the poem will make sense. When children are all standing in their lines, ask them to read the poem, each child reading their own line.

You Can... **Hold a poetry award**

Once all of your children have enjoyed reading poetry and exploring different ways of creating poetry, why not make a school or class poetry award? Consider the main benefit: all children will need to read a number of poems on the shortlist in order to vote for their favourite. Additional benefits will be that the status of poetry is raised in your class or school and that children begin to talk about poems.

Thinking points

● There are some logistical issues to consider such as how all children are going to manage to read the poems: you will need to have access to a substantial number of copies of the poems you intend to shortlist. Even if every class in the school contributes two poems to a shortlist, you will still need to make the poems available to everybody else. In order that you aren't infringing any copyright laws, you may wish to contact either the poet or the publisher and ask their permission to use their poem in your award. If the poem is already available on-line then direct children to the relevant web pages; check terms and conditions of the websites before displaying or printing material.

Tips, ideas and activities

● Even the most reluctant of readers is likely to want to contribute to a class or school award. This can't happen without the goodwill of the staff who will need to be prepared to make it an exciting event to encourage children to participate. However, with a little goodwill it can be an amazingly powerful event and, with staff support and enthusiasm, reluctant readers throughout the school should want to participate.

● You'll need to decide on categories. Are all the poems to be modern, accessible poems? (This may have the advantage of your being able to invite the winning poet to visit your school to collect their prize.) Or do you want to include some of the more traditional or more challenging poems?

● Before you begin you will need to create a panel of judges. This should be inclusive, in terms of reading attainment, age and gender. The judges will need to create the shortlist from all the nominated poems.

● Decide how the poems are to be introduced to the children. If it's a whole-school event, why not invite children to read their favourite poems in assembly before submitting them into the process?

● Clarify how many poems each class – or group of children if it's just your class – can nominate. Try to have a shortlist of no more than 5–10 poems.

● Check that all of the children understand the idea of voting. They won't all have their choice of poem selected and some of them might find that difficult.

● Once all of the poems for the shortlist have been selected, revisit the selection process within your class so that all of the children have the opportunity to hear all of the poems on the shortlist.

You Can... **Find out about authors**

Part of the process of becoming a reader is selecting the books that you read. In the very early stages of learning to read, it's often difficult to give children access to a choice of books, but as soon as it's appropriate, they should know how to make their own book choices. And for children, as for adults, part of that choice will depend on the author.

Thinking points

● In the overfull curriculum, it's too easy to lose opportunities to read aloud to your class. A class novel, however, is a critical experience for children to share with you and each other: for reluctant readers in particular, the class novel is the main point of access into the world of reading. Sharing a book together, finding out about its author, discussing the characters' actions and predicting future events is the basis of your reading community. Within this community, all members can feel included and for many children this is a formative experience.

● Think of the authors you were first introduced to in class novels at school. Can you remember the teacher who introduced you to a favourite author? Which authors would you like your children to remember you for?

Tips, ideas and activities

● Consider the character of the class you have at the moment. Different authors and different books will be more appropriate for different classes. Take account of children's concentration, their willingness to listen and to persevere with description, or their need for swift-moving action. Part of the excitement of a class novel is sharing it with each individual class.

● Select some books that you would like to share with your class. Introduce the books to children, including talking about each author and their other works. Give children opportunities to discuss the books and ask questions about them before voting which will be the next class novel.

● Use your school library service: ask them to put together a book box containing books by your chosen author. Allow children to read and share opinions on these books.

● Talk about children's expectations of the chosen author. *Is this author likely to write books about family life, animals or fighting? Do they write adventure stories, funny stories or non-fiction books and so on?* Use these conversations to help children to develop an understanding of different fiction genres and the difference between fiction and non-fiction books.

● Invite an author to come into school and talk about their work. Try visiting www.writingtogether.org.uk for advice on having a writer visit your school. Useful contacts for finding an author in your area include national organisations, such as the Arts Council England, National Literacy Trust, Scottish Book Trust, and local literacy festival organisers (such as Cheltenham, Oxford).

● Find out more about your favourite authors. Publishers' websites which have author biographies and interviews include www.scholastic.co.uk (The Zone), www.bloomsbury.com and www.orchardbooks.co.uk/links.htm (this gives links to individual authors' websites).

You Can... **Find out about illustrators**

For reluctant readers in particular, the illustrator controls access to a text. The child's first impression of the text will be through its illustrations. More often than not, we know the name of a book's author, but the name of the illustrator is often less well known. Help your children to appreciate the role of the illustrator.

Thinking points

● Do you encourage children to draw as part of the writing process? For some writers, the story begins in pictures, either those that they actually draw or those that they envision as a film strip. Perhaps enabling children to recognise the close links between words and pictures might help some of the reluctant readers and writers to engage.

● Book illustration is a fine art. There are an increasing number of pictures books written for older children – use them to demonstrate to children how the pictures can tell a story which adds to that of the author. A good illustrator does more than simply reflect the story: they can add a richness all of their own.

Tips, ideas and activities

● Select a number of picture books aimed at older children and illustrated by different illustrators. Ask the class to create their expectations of the book based only on the pictures. Talk about how the illustrator creates an expectation.

● Compare illustrations of characters on covers of books: how does the way the illustrator portrays the characters affect the reader? Do the same for settings.

● Give groups of children a few books which share the same illustrator. They could then explore how a theme is developed by the illustrator. Alternatively, give them a selection of books from different illustrators so they can establish the themes that a particular illustrator seems to excel at.

● Discuss the fact that illustrators, like authors, tend to find that their style matches certain themes better than others: some illustrators have very distinctive spiky styles which are less suitable for gentle domestic comedy, whereas others have rounded colourful styles which don't work so well in mystery stories.

● Find a variety of illustrated poetry anthologies and compare illustrations of poems from different illustrators.

● Give children opportunities to explore their own illustrative styles. Poems are ideal starting points as children can explore different themes and decide which kinds of poems they enjoy illustrating. Ask them to explain their choices.

● Encourage groups of children to do mini-projects on different illustrators whose work they admire.

● Invite an illustrator to come into school and talk about their work. Try visiting www.booktrusted.co.uk to find an illustrator who lives near you.

● Find out more about your favourite illustrators. Publishers' websites which have illustrator biographies include www.bloomsbury.com and www.orchardbooks.co.uk (this gives links to individual illustrators' websites).

You Can... **Write trailers for books**

TV and film trailers entice audiences by offering potential viewers snippets of information about the dramatic plot, characters and actors. Why not use this idea in your class for books too? Create a display trail of 'book trailers' which leads right into your school or class library.

Thinking points

● Creating 'trailers' for books can be a powerful way to entice children to read since trailers are short, punchy and ask questions rather than answer them. The aim of any TV or film trailer is to intrigue and to capture the imagination, thus creating a potential audience. What kind of information would a book trailer need to include in order to do the same job?

● Before you start children on developing a trail of book trailers, you need to consider what kinds of books you are going to encourage them to read. Are you limiting it to books by a certain author, to books in your library, to books within the genre you are studying? How can you ensure that your trailers are inclusive and entice your most difficult to reach children?

Tips, ideas and activities

● Begin by looking together at film trailers for films that children have watched and enjoyed. Sites like www.disney.co.uk, www.thefilmfactory.co.uk, www.warnerbros.co.uk and www.paramountpictures.co.uk have trailers of current and past films.

● As you watch different trailers, ask children to construct a chart and to list what kind of information is included in each trailer (information about plot, character, setting, cast, genre, for example). Discuss why each of the elements is included in the trailer. Ask children to evaluate and critique the trailers.

● Talk about how to translate each of the film elements into a book trailer. Do they think it's reasonable to replace the names of the famous actors with those of well-known authors?

● Consider a book or story you have all read together. Ask different groups of children to write playscripts and carry out dramatisations of their own book trailers. If you can, film them so that children can then evaluate and critique their own book trailers using the lists they drew up at the start.

● Talk about how to translate the dramatic scripts into brief written pieces. *What information must be included? Does the order in which the information is given make an impact?* Remind children that the book trailers are not book reviews; they serve a different function.

● Discuss presentation of the book trailers. *Does presentation matter? Should they be presented in colour or black and white? Handwritten or computer generated? Pinned onto a wall, written onto footprints on the floor or hung on mobiles from the ceiling?*

● Once children have negotiated their own ideas of what book trailers should look like, create monthly trails to your school or classroom library – ensuring that at least one copy of each book is available to borrow.

You Can... **Create a story world**

There are many ways of creating a story world in a classroom: from reading aloud, to guided or independent reading, to whole-class drama sessions. The important thing to do, however, is to give all readers – and especially reluctant readers – a glimpse inside the world of a good story.

Thinking points

● One of the joys of reading is entering another world created by a different person. Whether the author's creation is familiar, fantasy or historical, the reader should be drawn into this world and should believe in it absolutely. In a really satisfying read, the world and its characters take on an existence beyond the pages of the book so that the reader is filled with wonder about events and characters and is able to wander around the imaginary world away from the printed page: the story doesn't finish even when the book does.

● All too often, the reluctant reader's only insight into this world is through their engagement with soap operas, films or computer games. While these are valid experiences, they are much more passive than the experience of imagining the setting and characters in a good book.

Tips, ideas and activities

● Use your class novel as a starting point for explorations into the world created by the author. Since reading this book is a shared experience, children will be able to pool their ideas. This may well give confidence to those who are unused to having to articulate their mental images and thoughts.

● Depending on the novel you are reading, you will want to focus on different aspects of the story in your whole-class time. For example:

  ◦ Settings can be explored through, 2D and 3D art; creating a colour palette for the landscape; writing descriptions; creating yes/no quizzes of details not included in the book (for example, *is the sand hot? Is the water blue? Do trees grow tall?*); imagining the inside or outside of buildings; discussion or drama around how people might move around different aspects in the setting.

  ◦ Characters have traditionally been explored through character profiles, wanted posters, reading journals and hot-seating. You can extend children's thoughts about a character by asking them to consider how a character might respond to a given situation (not taken from the book); by exploring how a character might move; by trying out different voices for the character; by thinking about which animal a character most represents; by creating a collage of the character's thoughts and interests inside a profile of their head and face.

  ◦ Events, possible events and alternative events can be recorded through story boarding; creating retrospective plans of a story to show how events relate to each other; drama conventions which allow children to piece together a scene from a book, considering why each character came to be there and what impact the event is likely to have on that character's life; collaborative creation of potential storylines and plot developments.

● Crucially, teach children that stories jump off the page and into the mind of the reader. Understanding this bond between author and reader can sometimes persuade reluctant readers to try another reading experience.

You Can... Set up a book group

Book groups are fairly easy and cheap to set up in school. In the same way that adult book groups meet on a monthly basis so members can discuss their responses to a book, a school book group can also work this way. Borrow a set of books from the school library service or liaise with your local library and agree on a time and place for the book group to meet, and talk about books.

Thinking points

● A reading school is generally a school in which adults read as well as children. Have you ever considered trying to set up a book group for adults in your school? As a community of people who all work together, you probably know each other well enough for an honest and respectful exchange of viewpoints and opinions. The book group should be open to all adults who work in school, or who are employed by the school.

● Dinner times are often too busy for a staff book group, but people who are interested may well be willing to meet either after school once a month or perhaps in the evening. Sharing books shouldn't be too much of a problem either, since you all work in the same school.

Tips, ideas and activities

● Book groups can be a very powerful motivator for reading, since if the book is popular and is being talked about, then most children will want to participate at some level. In order to be truly inclusive, however, you may need to make specific arrangements for the books to be read aloud – in order that your reluctant readers can join in too.

● Most book groups meet on a monthly basis to discuss their chosen book. You may feel that this isn't sufficiently frequent to maintain momentum, but equally it's important that the 'meets' aren't so frequent that reading the books becomes a chore for children.

● The general pattern with book groups is that the participants take it in turn to select the books for the group to read. Depending on access to sets of books, this system may or may not suit your school group but do try and give children some sense of choice in the books they read. Their choice may not match yours, but if they are giving up their free time, their choice should override yours in this instance. The aim is to persuade children that reading something is a good use of their time.

● You might find it easier to agree some questions in advance so that children are looking out for opinions as they read their book. For reluctant readers in particular, you don't want to make children have to reread the book in order to be able to participate in discussions.

● Try to ensure that any questions asked of children are open-ended so that no more is needed for an appropriate response than to have read and considered the book. Try to avoid 'right' answers – if children feel that their answers are wrong they will soon decide that there are more important things to do with their time.

You Can... **Read for a purpose**

Why do you read? Why do you ask children in your class to read? What kinds of texts do you ask your reluctant readers to read? Is the purpose clear to them? Throughout this book there are many ideas about reading for a purpose, but here are a few more just to get you thinking.

Thinking points

● As literate people, we read all day long without even noticing it and we take accessing ideas and information through the written word entirely for granted. It's too easy to make assumptions about what children take for granted and it's entirely possible that some of your reluctant readers don't see the point in reading.

● When you set reading challenges for children, it may be worthwhile occasionally asking children why they think you are asking them to read. Is it for practice, so they can get better at reading? It is to keep them quiet while you do something else? Do you want them to find information – and if so what do you want them to do with the information once they've found it? Sometimes, clarifying the purpose for reading will encourage children to have a go.

Tips, ideas and activities

● Reading for enjoyment is unlikely to be high on the list of priorities of a reluctant reader, but most children will attempt reading for some purpose. Are these children reading to follow instructions? To play their computer games? To find out where things are kept? To find out about a hobby? Or are they only reluctant readers when they are in the classroom?

● Talk to your Key Stage 1 colleagues and ask for permission to borrow resources, particularly reading books. Publishers are increasingly publishing non-fiction books which are ostensibly aimed at Key Stage 1, but which recognise the probability of Key Stage 2 children reading them too. This means that the designs and presentations are often appropriate for Key Stage 2 children.

● Find books and on-line resources which develop the child's own interests: if a child enjoys magic tricks, track down simple texts which teach magic tricks; if they like art, find books on different artists.

● Organise a writers' workshop. Allocate one afternoon a week which centres on writing and research for writing. Allow children to select their own topic and give them access to the school library and on-line resources. Create an expectation that all children will research and then write. Your reluctant readers may need support, but if they can select their own subject they are more likely to participate. (Ensure they choose something they would like to find out more about, rather than something they are already an expert on.)

● Ask for responses to a class humanities topic to be in the form of researched presentations including handmade artefacts. Beyond an introduction to establish prior knowledge, give minimal input to the class, but give them adequate time to research in pairs or small groups and to make their artefacts. At the end of the time, ask all children to contribute to a presentation on their chosen topic. Even your reluctant readers may feel able to contribute since the clear purpose to their reading/research is an oral presentation.

You Can... **Make an information tool kit**

If you can make reading for information both 'cool' and easy, you are more likely to encourage your reluctant readers. By giving these children their own easily accessible 'information tool kits' you can both teach them the skills they need to find information quickly and efficiently and give them the tools they need to do it.

Thinking points

● An information tool kit needs to match the needs of its owner – and you. It should be a short-term intervention to help to focus the child's mind and attention on developing skills for learning. If the child starts to misuse the tool kit, or if you don't give the child time and opportunities to use it, the tool kit will lose its value very quickly.

● Small tool boxes or open carry cases can be found in DIY stores. As long as the case is large enough to hold the tools you need, but not too bulky, this kind of container is ideal – especially for boys.

Tips, ideas and activities

● Ensure that all the items in the tool kit will be useful to children during the course of the day (although all of the tools won't be needed all day long). All tool kits should include a pencil and a pencil sharpener, colouring pencils, together with a small whiteboard, dry-wipe marker pen and wiper. Sticky notes can also be helpful as children can use them for noting down thoughts (for example when planning for writing) and for communicating with you and the other children.

● Key Stage 2 children will respond very well to handheld electronic spell-checkers. These are no longer prohibitively expensive and encourage children to check their spelling. Many reluctant readers won't use a dictionary, but they will often use a spell-checker. Spell-checkers have the additional advantage of providing a range of interactive word games, such as hangman and anagrams. Once you have taught children how to access and play these games, encourage their use during unstructured times in the classroom. This can have a beneficial impact on behaviour.

● Additional books such as an easy encyclopaedia, dictionary and thesaurus are important parts of a tool kit (as long as the child has been taught to use them). Also include at least one information book, with good pictures, on a subject which interests the child.

● A laminated A4 mat should also be included (see illustration). Depending on the stage of the child, it may have: letters of the alphabet with pictures; high-frequency words; spelling and reading rules; reminders of the current Individual Education Plan (IEP) targets.

● Give opportunities to use the tool kit frequently during the school day in order to make the child feel important and to give opportunities for using and developing reading skills.

You Can... Understand information texts

Reading an information text – whether in print or on-screen – requires different skills from reading fiction texts. Many reading schemes now include non-fiction books as a part of their offering, and these are often appropriate for reading with your reluctant readers as they are designed to be high interest and exciting but with more limited and accessible texts.

Thinking points

● Non-fiction texts are often good texts for reluctant and struggling readers and you will often find that children can read more difficult non-fiction texts than they can fiction texts. It may be a generalisation, but many boys are less interested in stories than girls.

● Non-fiction texts, with the exception of the more narrative recounts and historical reports, have a number of features which make them appropriate for reluctant readers of both genders: even difficult non-fiction books can be highly illustrated, so the reluctant reader doesn't feel that their book looks any different from the other children's books. In non-fiction texts children can get information from different sources, so a visual learner can read a diagram, a map or a graph; they often don't have to remember a sequence of events, since the information given is generally in short sections.

Tips, ideas and activities

● Teach children how to 'pre-read' a non-fiction book by finding information from the book title, cover images and blurb. They should then turn to the contents page and find as much information as they can from it.

● Before children continue past the contents page, teach them to pause and to consider questions such as:
  ● What am I looking for in this book? Will it give me the information I am searching for? Is this likely to be the appropriate book?
  ● What do I already know about this topic? Is this book likely to increase my knowledge? Will it answer any questions I have?

● Once children have determined that the book is relevant, check that they know key differences between the contents page and the index. Do they understand how these are organised? Can they use both to find information?

● Once children have found the page(s) they need to look at, teach them to make a mental map of the information on the pages. This should include:
  ● Looking at the different information sources on the pages: are they all likely to give the same information? If so, which are most likely to be useful and efficient to read?
  ● Using the headings and sub-headings to consider the likely contents of each paragraph
  ● Using the topic sentence of each paragraph (see page 22).

● Teach children how to use skimming and scanning to find information:
  ● Skimming involves getting a brief overview by a quick read of headings, sub-headings and topic sentences.
  ● Scanning involves looking for key words and reading around the text in which they are found.

You Can... **Develop language to discuss information books**

Readers need to be able to talk about the books they have read. This often involves learning a technical language, particularly when it comes to describing non-fiction books. However, once children have learned the language, it gives them a feeling of being an insider and they can take pride in contributing their ideas and observations.

Thinking points

● There is always a debate as to how much technical language children should be taught. The experience of many teachers, however, is that if children are able to understand the concept being taught, then they will often enjoy learning and using the correct term for that concept. Not only does it make them feel very adult, but it also gives them access to being an 'expert' because this is the language that experts use. You will know your reluctant readers well enough to know what they can cope with and which terms are most important to them.

● The other big advantage of giving children access to technical language is that it makes it so much easier for class discussions: if you can all use the same term to refer to the same concept, it saves misunderstandings and time.

Tips, ideas and activities

● Teach children the idea that every piece of writing has an audience and purpose. Read texts together to try to work out why the author wrote the text and who it is aimed at. Looking for clues to answer these questions can be a motivating factor for children.

● Give children a checklist so that they know the key purposes of the different text types they might read. For example:
   ● Report: describes how things are. Written in the present tense.
   ● Historical report: describes how things were. Written in the past tense.
   ● Recount (including biography and autobiography): relates incidents within the life of a person – generally written in the first person, but biographies and newspaper articles are often in the third person. Uses sequencing language.
   ● Explanation: describes a process. Uses the language of cause and effect.
   ● Persuasion (including advertisements): tries to influence the reader to believe something. Uses language both of sequencing and cause and effect.
   ● Argument and discussion: presents all the sides of an issue, with greater or lesser bias. Uses language both of sequencing and cause and effect.
   ● Instruction: tells the reader to do something or how to do something. Written in the second person and uses imperative (command) verbs.

● In addition to teaching children to recognise the text types, (which often gives clues to the audience and purpose of a text) teach them the technical language to talk about the non-fiction books that they read so they can tell you where they found the information, for example: *main text, bullet points, caption, illustration, image, label, diagram, flow chart, map.*

You Can... **Follow instructions**

The ability to read, to understand and to follow instructions is an important life skill. Instructional texts are commonly studied as a text type, but too often this is children's only experience of reading instructions and it can be a limited experience for reluctant readers. But reading instructions can be fun and motivating.

Thinking points

● Instructional texts can be comparatively easy to read, since it is not uncommon for step-by-step instructions to be illustrated. However, some of the instructional texts aimed at the school market are more focused on ensuring that all of the text type features are included than on the content, so the texts can be demotivating and may not compel children to read.

● It is important for children to understand the language and purpose of instructional texts because they surround us in our daily lives. Teach children to recognise that notices like 'No parking' and 'Queue here' are instructional texts, as are lists of classroom or school rules. Teachers often focus on the organisation of chronological instructional texts, but non-chronological texts are as important to understand.

Tips, ideas and activities

● Can your children remember and follow instructions given orally? Before you ask them to read and remember instructions, see how many spoken instructions they can remember. If memory inhibits them from following instructions effectively, give them strategies for reading and following instructions.

● There are a myriad of motivating instructional texts available which you can look at with your children: look at comics, puzzle books, construction kits, and 'how to' books, including books about magic tricks, origami or crystal growing sets. If you think laterally, you can find texts that will appeal to all of your children.

● Ask children to bring in instructional texts from home. Compare the value of, for example, flat-pack furniture or LEGO® set instructions which are often wordless.

● Find and view a picture which has a lot of busy detail in it: www.theartwolf.com/services/wallpapers.htm is a good place to start. Write instructions which children have to follow to find particular details in the picture.

● Let groups of children write instructions for others to follow as they search for clues in pictures.

● Take the opportunity of any school fund-raising event to employ your reluctant readers as sign writers.

● Walk round the school looking for evidence of instructional texts. Ask children to read notices and labels on walls and displays. Check that they know that they are looking for imperative (command) verbs rather than numbers since many environmental print instructions are not written as numbered lists.

● Try to set up a liaison with a younger class for an afternoon when your reluctant readers take charge of playing a board game with a group of younger children. Allow your children to read the instructions carefully before they play the game so that they will know how to help the younger ones.

You Can... Visit a public library

When did you last visit the public library closest to your school – or the one which children are most likely to have access to? Most libraries today – including travelling libraries – are anxious to encourage more children to join and are setting themselves up with activities and resources to encourage all youngsters.

Thinking points

● Before you take your class to the library, visit it yourself. This isn't just for the purpose of doing a risk assessment, but also so that you are prepared for the kinds of resources and activities available to children in the library. If it is possible, try to organise a children's librarian from the county or borough to join you in the library: they are often more used to presenting their library to children than the librarians who work there.

● Before you leave, ask for a pile of membership forms. If you take them back to school and have them signed by children's parents, then return them to the library before your visit, children can often be presented with their very own library cards when you go to the library together.

Tips, ideas and activities

● If you are lucky enough to have a school library, visit it with children before you visit your local library. Explore the kinds of books available: is there both fiction and non-fiction? If so, talk about how the books are shelved: it is important that children know that if they take a book off a shelf in a library, they can't just put it back on the nearest shelf. Discuss with them why they think libraries are arranged in this way.

● Establish appropriate behaviours in the library: although public libraries no longer insist on silence, they probably expect that voices will be muted to allow other library users to concentrate – and they will certainly discourage rushing around or eating and drinking near the books.

● Ask a group of reluctant readers to organise the books in your classroom as they would expect to find books organised in the library. Allow opportunities for children to browse through the books. In many classrooms, there are too many books so children only ever look at a small number. (In some schools, classroom book stocks are limited to about 50–60 books in the classroom which are changed every half-term so that all of the books are available at some point.)

● Encourage children and their parents to make use of the library once you have visited as a class. Advertise activity sessions in the holidays and weekend activities; take time to look at books borrowed from the library which support the curriculum; encourage parents to borrow books to share with their children and to encourage reluctant readers to read.

● As library membership dwindles, libraries are closing down. Help to reverse this trend by making sure that all of your children are members of the library and that they know where the nearest library is. Libraries are a vital resource in a community and schools need to play their part in promoting their use.

You Can... **Find out about reading habits**

Why do you read? Why do you think children in your class read? Try doing a survey to see what children understand of their own reading habits. In the same way that you teach children different purposes for writing, it is important to recognise the different purposes for reading. Once you know why they choose to read, you can begin to incorporate opportunities into your own lessons.

Thinking points

● Children who can read, but choose not to, are much less worrying than those who can't read and choose not to engage with the process. Those who can read, but choose not to, are losing out on ideas that can enrich their personal lives; those whose reluctance masks a refusal to engage are potentially losing out on their futures. These are the children, above all, who we need to draw into reading.

● Do you know *why* there are children in your class who don't want to learn to read? By the time they are aged seven or older, poor self-esteem and an unwillingness to try something that they already know they will 'fail' at, are often key reasons. For this reason, it is crucial that you make appropriate provision of texts which are progressive and supportive, but not demeaning. Above all, don't let them read books from the same reading scheme as their more successful younger siblings.

Tips, ideas and activities

● Make time to hold at least termly 'reading conversations' with your reluctant readers in particular. This is a timetabled opportunity to talk to children about reading. During this, you aim to find out about them as readers. For example:

- When, where and for what purposes do they read?
- What do they like/dislike about reading?
- What challenges do they face? If, for example, you find that a child has a phobia about reading any word with more than five letters, that can give you clear guidance for your future planning.
- Would they like to be able to read? Why/why not?
- What do they see as their immediate targets in developing as a reader?
- What do they think your role is in supporting them? Is there anything that they would like you to do or not to do that might help them to read?

● It is often more effective to try to have a real conversation rather than a question and answer session. When children feel under pressure their answers may reflect what they think you want to hear, whereas in the context of a more relaxed conversation they are more likely to feel relaxed and offer their real views.

● Once children have had one reading conversation with you, they will know what kind of thoughts to prepare for the next one. Although they are time-consuming, termly reading conversations give you a real chance to support your reluctant readers in the most appropriate and time-efficient ways in between these conversations.

● Use these conversations as part of your assessment profile of each of your reluctant readers. Over time, they will reveal a profile which can be used to trigger interventions.

You Can... **Set up treasure hunts**

Most children enjoy treasure hunts and find them very motivating and exciting. They are often best done outside in the warmer weather, rather than indoors. Organising a treasure hunt can seem like a lot of work but if you laminate your clues and plan them carefully, they can be recycled and reused in a different order.

Thinking points

● Before you plan a treasure hunt there are some obvious issues to consider around children's safety and supervision and these factors are likely to determine the extent of the treasure hunt you can create. Will, for example, your whole class be outside all at the same time, or will you be sending them out in small groups alone with a trusted adult?

● To some extent, the opportunities afforded by your outside space will also limit your activities. City-centre schools with tarmac playgrounds will be the base for a different kind of treasure hunt from suburban and country schools with extensive playing fields or adventure playgrounds. However, none of these constraints affect your ability to organise a treasure hunt for your children - they just impact on the space and places you can use.

Tips, ideas and activities

● Treasure hunts can take place in as small a space as a tray of sand and as large a space as a whole school grounds.

● Consider how you are going to present the clues: are they all going to be on one sheet, or are you going to place the next set of clues at each location so children only have one set to follow at a time?

● Classroom or playground treasure hunts can be simple or complex:
  ○ Take several photographs of a soft toy sitting in an easily identified place. Place an instruction beside the first photograph which will guide children to find the next photograph and so on (for example: 'Find photograph 2 under the carpet').
  ○ Match clues to photographs (for example: 'Inside a brown pot with a hole in the bottom'). Then ask children to find the object and another clue.
  ○ Make treasure trails which involve an orienteering-type of activity: children read an instruction at one location, then follow it to the next location where they find another instruction. At each location, as well as the new instruction, children should expect to find some evidence to show that they found the location. This could involve finding a letter; using a particular colour pen which has been placed at that location; collecting a small object from each location and so on.

● Ideally, in a treasure hunt, children should expect to find part of the treasure at each place. They will then need to use all of the separate 'treasures' to solve some kind of a puzzle.

You Can... Set up a book quiz

Research from the National Literacy Trust suggests that many boys – including those who are reluctant readers – are motivated to read by competition and challenge. Holding class or school book quizzes can be a way of creating competition, which allows your reluctant readers to compete and succeed.

Thinking points

● Before you set up your own book quiz, check with your school library service or local library to see if they have already produced book quizzes. If they have, their quiz might form the basis of your own, but if this is your reluctant readers' first experience of book quizzes, you will need to check that they can access all of the books in the list.

● Many library services also encourage inter-school book quizzes. At first, these may not be appropriate for your reluctant readers, but raising the profile and status of reading in your class and school may well have a knock-on effect in motivating all children to read and participate.

Tips, ideas and activities

● Book quizzes can be done at many levels:
  ○ At their simplest, let children who are reading together in a guided reading group search for details in the text and ask other children questions at the end of the guided reading session.
  ○ Groups of children can build their questions during several guided reading sessions so that more books are involved in the quiz.
  ○ Pairs and individual children can write questions as they read other books during the day; your book quiz might happen informally at the end of a school day or more formally on a designated afternoon.
  ○ Alternatively, you may prefer an open quiz where children take the quiz paper away with them and have a week or so to complete it. (This type of quiz makes an ideal sponsored event for fund-raising).

● Children can either be in teams competing against each other (in the manner of a pub quiz team) or you can ask questions of the whole class, or you can give a written question sheet.

● If at all possible, involve children in creating their book quiz. As long as a wide variety of children are able to participate in creating the quiz, then no one will have any particular advantage in answering the questions.

● Draw up lists of books which will form the basis for a quiz. You might want to grade or colour-code the books so that all children can read from an appropriate selection of books.

● Discuss with children what appropriate questions might be like. In a quiz, they are less likely to be questions about what the reader thinks, and more likely to be about what the author explicitly said. Allow questions which are based on deduction (when there are clues in the text) but not those based on inference (when you have to read between the lines).

● Ensure that you have sufficient copies of all of the books so that all children can be involved.

You Can... Introduce paired reading partnerships

In the crowded curriculum, particularly at Key Stage 2, it is often difficult for teachers to listen to all children reading individually as well as in groups. By creating a regular reading partnership of older and younger children, the little ones build up a relationship with their 'reading mentor' or 'reading buddy' and the older children learn some responsibility – as well as rehearsing their reading skills.

Thinking points

● There is a lot of anecdotal evidence to suggest that struggling and reluctant older readers are often the best reading mentors. They have generally struggled to some degree with learning to read and so are often in the best position to offer advice to younger struggling and reluctant readers.

● In a 30-minute paired reading session, you could reasonably expect the younger child to read their book to the older child and the older child to read a book to their younger partner. Encourage your less confident readers to practise and rehearse the book of their choice so that they can read confidently when it's their turn. For this, you will need to ensure that they have access to appropriate books.

Tips, ideas and activities

● Work closely with your colleague whose class you are going to read with in order to ensure that the pairings of children are appropriate. Generally, your highest achieving readers should read with the younger high achievers while your reluctant readers are likely to work more confidently with the less confident younger readers.

● Invite the teacher of the younger children to come and train your children to work with the younger ones. Your children will need to know, for example:
  ○ When and how to intervene if the younger child hesitates, misreads a word or gets stuck and needs help;
  ○ If the younger child is still using phonics as their only reading strategy, your children will need to know how to help the younger children to 'sound out' their words.
  ○ If other reading strategies have been introduced, your children will need to have some understanding as to what they are and how to prompt effectively.
  ○ Are your children going to engage in discussion about the book? They may need to be prompted as to what kinds of questions to ask. Some children find it difficult to think of questions which search for comprehension, so they may need practice at doing this as they read themselves.
  ○ Is there any expectation that your children will keep or contribute to a record of the reading experience? If so, what will this be?

● Paired reading can be a very effective reading intervention, as well as a positive experience, for both older and younger children. However, be aware as you supervise the session of whether children are remaining focused. Sometimes, it's useful to arrange paired reading every week just in the second half of each term in order to keep the experience fresh and useful.

You Can... Do the Summer Reading Challenge

Every year, there are national summer reading challenges which are organised and run by public libraries. These challenges involve thousands of children in reading. Are your children involved? If not, your local library will be pleased to give you leaflets about the challenge. If you can't or don't want to participate in a nationally organised reading challenge, why not run a school one instead?

Thinking points

- Reading challenges appeal to many children, including reluctant readers, as there is a clear goal and generally a reward at the end. If you are holding the challenge during the summer holidays, you may want to organise the celebration for the autumn term so that all children know that their current teacher will be able to follow their progress through into the start of the next year. This is particularly an issue for children who are about to transfer into secondary school. It is important that reluctant readers in this category are encouraged to develop their reading over the summer in order that they don't lose momentum, but the reading challenge won't mean anything unless children know that their efforts will be rewarded and appreciated. Can you liaise with secondary school teachers and get their support for a celebration either in your school, or in the secondary school?

Tips, ideas and activities

- Find information about Summer Reading Challenges from:
  - National Literacy Trust Website (www.literacytrust.org.uk)
  - Their Reading Futures (www.theirreadingfutures.org.uk)
  - The Reading Agency (www.readingagency.org.uk)

- Whether you are organising your own reading challenge or participating in a national event, a whole-school challenge is by far the most effective as it involves the whole school community.

- If you are holding the challenge in school, consider:
  - What the rewards will be;
  - How children should record their reading. This needs to be a high quality resource as it shows how much you value the reading challenge.
  - What the expectation is, for example:
    - Making a list of books I've read and adding to it.
    - Reading other children's book recommendations.
    - Reading comics.
    - Reading books suggested on a list.
    - Reading anything I want to.
    - Reading for next term's school project.
    - Reading everything by one author.
    - Reading around a topic that interests me.
    - Reading more books than anyone else.

- You know your school community, so you will know about involving all families whatever their culture, language or knowledge about reading. You will have to make decisions about which language you want children to read in; you should ensure access arrangements for any child who needs assistive technology; you may also need to consider how to include traveller children and recent immigrants. All schools will also need to consider how to include struggling readers. Look for ideas at: www.readingrockets.org

You Can... Help parents to read with their children

Evidence from the National Literacy Trust suggests that adults and teenagers, looking back at their own reading experiences, generally identify Mum as being the person who was most influential in their success in reading. This evidence is important when considering how we can engage children with reading: often, the first step is to engage their parents.

Thinking points

● Do you know the reading backgrounds of children in your class? How supportive and involved are their parents? If you feel that the parents are not as involved as you would like them to be, it may be worth considering why not.

● Which language do you ask your children to read in at home? If English is not their first language, or the language of their parents, why not offer them appropriate books in their first language? Evidence from around the world suggests that encouraging proficiency in a child's first language benefits their learning of English. Certainly, if the parents don't speak English, they will find it difficult to encourage their children to learn in English.

Tips, ideas and activities

● How are you most likely to reach your children's parents? Will it be through a presentation, through individual discussions, through letters, leaflets or bookmarks?

● How do your parents react when invited onto the school premises? Some parents have negative feelings about school because they themselves didn't have positive schooling. If you need to encourage those parents to listen to you talk about supporting their children's reading, you might want to consider holding the meeting away from school. The back room or upstairs rooms of local pubs and clubs can make very good, informal and unthreatening venues.

● Are children's parents literate and, if so, in which language? If the parents can read, booklets such as the ones on pages 59–62 may be helpful in giving parents advice in supporting their children. Ask members of the local community to translate the booklets into an appropriate language.

● Make and laminate bookmarks, based on the information in the booklets from pages 60 and 62. Slip a bookmark into a book when you send it home with the child. The bookmark will list the key strategies that the child is using to read and you can use a chinagraph pencil to tick those that you want the child and their parent to focus on. Being able to refer to the bookmark for guidance will make parents feel involved and supported in helping their child to read.

● Ask children how they think their parents could support them more in their reading. Children will certainly know whether or not their parents can read and in which language. Some children may be able to articulate how they would like to be helped at home.

● Start a Dads 'n' Lads reading club. Boys like to have male role models who read with them. Dads 'n' Lads clubs are now popular in many areas and they are empowering dads to share their reading habits with their sons.

You Can... **Use ideas from the National Literacy Trust**

Have you ever used resources from the National Literacy Trust (NLT)? Their website at www.literacytrust.org.uk has a host of ideas, information, free leaflets and links to useful organisations whose aim is to promote literacy in schools and at home.

Thinking points

● The National Literacy Trust is a charity which produces free materials and campaigns for their use in school. Your reluctant readers are precisely the children that the NLT is most concerned about, so have a look at the website and see what you can gain from it. NLT initiatives include Reading Connects, Reading Champions, Reading Angels and the Family Reading Campaign.

● The National Literacy Trust is an independent charity that 'changes lives through literacy'. It is also responsible for organising initiatives both in schools and in the wider community, including some for the DCSF.

● The main concern of the National Literacy Trust is that 20% of the UK adult population still struggles to read and write. If your reluctant readers have parents who are in that 20%, then there is a real danger that your reluctant readers will become part of the next generation of people who struggle to read and write.

Tips, ideas and activities

● Find out whether your school is eligible for support from the Reading is Fundamental (RIF) project, which provides books to children in disadvantaged areas. In order to gain support you have to apply to run a RIF project in your school and be committed to doing some fund-raising of your own – this includes organising a team of volunteers from the local community to select books for children to choose from and to hold some kind of event to promote the books.

● The Family Reading Campaign provides activity cards, certificates for 'Reading Families', posters, ideas, activities, weblinks and so on that you can use to support your own community. The activity cards are aimed at parents of children at different ages and stages in reading, from babies upwards. You can even download editable versions of the cards so that you can personalise them for your school. The originals are available in a number of languages.

● Reading the Game is an initiative run by the NLT and the Premier League to promote reading, writing and speaking and listening through the power of sport. Posters showing football players reading and talking about reading may give reluctant readers that little boost of motivation.

You Can... **Encourage RIBIT**

Reading in Bed is Terrific (RIBIT) has proved to be a powerful intervention in both Australia and the USA and is now making an impact in the UK. The idea is simple: children read a book, or part of a book, aloud or to themselves in bed at night; their parents sign to witness the fact that the reading has been done; once children have read a certain number of times, they are given a certificate.

Thinking points

● Children have traditionally read in bed at night. These days, however, there are often TVs, DVDs and computer consoles in children's bedrooms and fewer and fewer children are reading in bed. RIBIT attempts to reinstate this reading habit.

● Reading in bed is a very psychologically strong activity. For most children, bed is associated with comfort and happiness, so when they read in bed the act of reading becomes comfortable and relaxed by association. In addition, reading in bed makes the brain focus on reading last thing at night; there is evidence to suggest that during the night, the brain continues to work on challenges which were present just before sleep.

Tips, ideas and activities

● Find out more about RIBIT at www.frogstone.com/maple_ridge/reading.asp. RIBIT can be individualised to your school and made more or less formal. Ideas from some primary schools who are already running the scheme in UK include:

  ● Giving each child an individualised booklist (generally compiled according to the reading attainment of the child). When children have finished a book, they are given a RIBIT sticker. When they finish 50 books, they can exchange their RIBIT stickers for a £5 book token.

  ● Each child on the scheme has a folder in the library. Within the folder is their booklist together with 'response pages' for each book read. Once children have read the book, they complete the response sheet and are given a voucher. When they have received 50 vouchers, they are allowed to select a book from a collection purchased and kept in school. (The school generally uses concessionary books from book fairs as the RIBIT free books).

  ● A group of parents can administer the RIBIT scheme: children enrol with permission from their parents and are then allowed to select books from a special 'RIBIT library' collection which is managed by the parents. When children return their book, they have a brief reading conference with one of the parent volunteers who asks them general questions about their response to the book. The child is then given a stamp on a card. When they have collected ten stamps, they can have a certificate; after five certificates they have a voucher to spend at a school book fair.

● RIBIT is easily adaptable to meet your school's needs. You need to consider:

  ● Whether the scheme will be open to all children.
  ● How to reward children for reading.
  ● How to finance the rewards.

You Can... **Support the Six Book Challenge**

The Six Book Challenge is run by the Reading Agency, in partnership with the National Literacy Trust. It is aimed primarily at adults who are working to improve their own literacy levels. The challenge – which is to read six books – runs from January to May each year and is supported by libraries.

Thinking points

- High levels of adult literacy make it easier for children to learn about reading in the home. Conversely, if there are low levels of adult literacy in the home, it can be very difficult for children to understand why people would ever bother to learn to read. If their role models can't or won't read, why should the children? This not only has a knock-on effect on children's literacy, but it also impacts on home-school relationships since so much communication is by the written word.

    If we can support our children's parents as they try to improve their own literacy, that should impact on children and their attitude and attainment in reading.

Tips, ideas and activities

- Do you know how many of your parents struggle with literacy? How many of them would benefit from support with reading? In our society, it's still something that adults often don't want to admit to or to talk about, but given that the potential impact on their children is so great it is useful if schools can establish honest and open dialogue with parents around their own literacy.

- The level of support you can offer to parents will vary enormously depending on the support and resources already available locally and other calls on your school's budget for work within the community. But some ideas of things you can possibly do to support the Six Book Challenge include the following:

    - Set up a book group specifically for the challenge in school. It doesn't need to be run by you – it can be run by any member of the community. Some members of non-teaching staff might themselves be grateful for the opportunity to improve their reading skills.
    - Make space on your school library shelves for books to be borrowed by adults reading for the challenge.
    - Invest in some books for adults reading towards the challenge. These can be sourced at www.firstchoicebooks.org.uk, a site organised and managed by the Reading Agency, who select and commission books aimed at adult emergent readers.
    - Become a 'Learning Provider' and run the challenge. Look at the Six Book Challenge website for more details about what is involved: wwwsixbookchallenge.org.uk.

- It's not your sole responsibility to spread literacy throughout the community, but often it takes one person's energies to start a scheme up before a member of the local community can be persuaded to continue running the group.

You Can... Agree targets with children

By the time children are in Key Stage 2, their feelings about themselves as readers are often confused with issues around self-esteem and confidence. If you give them a clear idea of the route forward, which they recognise, this will enable them to be better readers. Otherwise, they may not be willing to make the effort required.

Thinking points

● Learning involves risk taking: you are always risking the possibility of failure as you strive to learn something new. If children are not sufficiently confident to be prepared to take risks, they are likely to grind to a halt with their learning. It is worth bearing this in mind as you negotiate targets with children, because understanding the child's attitude to learning will help you to agree appropriate targets.

● Ideally, target setting will evolve out of a diagnostic reading session and a reading conversation (see page 43). This will give you a clear idea of where children are with their reading, where they want to be and the steps that will be needed to help them to achieve that goal.

Tips, ideas and activities

● Create targets collaboratively with children. As a wealth of research suggests, children are more likely to achieve targets that they have been involved in setting. This seems to makes sense: if a child has decided on their target then it can be assumed that the child has some understanding of what achieving that target might involve.

● In order for a child to make progress, the teacher and child first need to establish at which stage the child is with their learning. They then need to agree where the child wants to get to and agree how they are going to bridge this gap. Since assessment for learning is now meant to drive planning forwards in the classroom, the implication is that all learners should be beginning to take some responsibility for their own learning: that responsibility has to involve developing an understanding of what it means to make progress.

● Work with the child to create a reading bridge or a reading ladder. Write the agreed goal at one end and the current state of affairs at the other. In no more than about five steps in between, agree what the small steps will be if the child is to achieve their goal. Let the child keep this document and cross off or colour in each small step as it's achieved.

● It is useful to start the target setting process by offering targets that the child is very close to achieving already. If they can tick off a target very quickly, they are likely to feel more positive towards the process of working with targets.

You Can... Set targets for improvement

Agreeing targets is just the first stage of an ongoing process and once the targets are in place, you need to monitor progress towards them: targets are unlikely to be met if the target setting process happens once a term and then targets are unmonitored and forgotten about. However, target setting and monitoring can be time-consuming so in order for it to yield results, the process established does need to be streamlined and useful.

Thinking points

● Consider how the target setting process happens in school at the moment. Are all children routinely involved in the process of setting and evaluating targets or is this something you will need to do individually and just with your reluctant readers? It is important to be aware of the practicalities of monitoring targets before you get involved in work with your reluctant readers: the process will only be successful if you are committed to it and have conviction that it will be a positive learning experience.

● For most reluctant readers, there will be a number of potentially useful targets. Sometimes, the problem is deciding which to address next. As well as giving the child some choice (see page 52), you should make sure that it will be possible for them to achieve whichever target they select by ensuring that all the choices reflect what you are going to teach. For example, don't give options of targets relating to reading stories if you are about to teach a poetry unit.

Tips, ideas and activities

● Where will you keep children's targets? In Key Stage 2, most schools put targets on special target cards, on flaps in children's books, on the front of reading records, on a reading bookmark or on a laminated sheet. Wherever you choose to put them, the targets are likely to be most successful if:

- They are in sight, so the child keeps on being reminded that they exist. Targets on an IEP in a file quickly get forgotten.
- They are continually read, so the child is constantly reminded what they are trying to achieve: perhaps establish a regularly slot in the week where targets are reviewed and updated if necessary.
- They are written in child-friendly language, so the child understands what they mean.
- They are somewhere where they can easily be replaced as they are achieved. If a child has achieved a target, they need fairly immediate feedback and congratulations, quickly followed by new negotiated targets. This keeps the child on-message and motivated. Targets written in or attached to exercise books are often easier to update and, kept in this way, are also specific to individual learners.

● Keeping a record of targets achieved is also invaluable for your reluctant reader, because they can see how many targets they have achieved. Spending a few minutes, every now and again, reading through the list of targets achieved can make a child feel very positive about continuing to strive towards their new targets.

● Try to keep to targets that can be achieved at least once within a week, particularly for reluctant readers, so that children can easily see that they are making progress. You can gradually increase the length of time for working towards a target, but the more they can be seen to achieve the better for children's motivation and self-confidence.

● If you need to go back and revisit a target that has already been marked as achieved, try to rephrase it using different words so the child doesn't get a feeling of regression.

You Can... Choose activities to reach your targets

Once targets are in place, there's a balancing act to be achieved: you have selected the most important skills to focus on from a number of possibilities, but does that mean that all teaching activities should now narrowly address the target or should you still be delivering a broader reading curriculum?

Thinking points

- You will know children in your own class better than anyone else in school, so you will know best how to motivate them. Some children need to know that all of their energies are directed towards their specific target and will resist activities which they perceive as being irrelevant; for those children you may want to review the targets soon and see if they should be replaced by more general targets, otherwise your teaching may have to become very narrowly focused.

- Activities for reluctant readers need to take place within the context of the activities for all the other children in your class, so there is a tension between activities which isolate one child or a group of children and those which are inclusive, support a useful aspect of reading, but do not directly address the chosen target. Teaching with individual targets is easier if you know your children well and determine the targets appropriately.

Tips, ideas and activities

- Research has repeatedly shown that narrowly teaching towards a specific target does not necessarily mean that the target is achieved. Narrow teaching often leads to narrow learning, where the child may appear to acquire a skill in one discrete context, but they may not be able to apply that skill across the curriculum contexts.

- Not all targets can be approached in the same way. A target which asks that a child reads a number of times a week, will need different activities from a target that asks a child to learn to split words into syllables, or one requiring them to learn to recognise high-frequency words. When you are agreeing targets, it is worth bearing in mind how you are going to support the child in reaching them.

- Successful teaching towards reading targets would generally require that the target is achieved several times (minimum of three) in a variety of different contexts.

- In order to support children's self-esteem, try to set activities which are consistent with those that the other children are engaged in; for example, give activities to support phonics while the other children are spelling rather then when they are doing reading comprehension.

- Broader teaching activities, where children are encouraged to make progress in a general skills area, can be more productive as children are presented with a variety of different approaches to meeting their target. So, for example, if a child's target is to read words with adjacent consonants, any kind of activity which involves reading, hearing or recognising adjacent consonants, manipulating letters in spelling games or reading comprehension of simple sentences will support the child in reaching the target.

- Where possible, use cross-curricular activities to teach around a target. By the time they are in Key Stage 2, children need to understand that reading and literacy skills are useful across the curriculum.

You Can... **Evaluate an intervention**

Any intervention can be expensive, not just in cash terms but also in view of the fact that by choosing to implement one intervention you are implicitly deciding not to try a different one which might benefit other children. It is always worth considering whether or not the intervention you chose was successful and whether or not you would try the same thing another time or how you would vary it.

Thinking points
● What kinds of interventions do you have in place to support your reluctant readers? Intervention can mean anything from differentiated targets, to an IEP, to individual or small group work, to implementing a published programme. For different children in different classrooms and schools, different interventions are successful. But no matter what you choose, doing something different is an intervention which really needs to be evaluated, however informal the process.

● Evaluating the impact of different treatments on reluctant readers is tricky because the outcome may not be measurable in terms of progress towards the next P-level or National Curriculum sub-level. The immediate impact may well be much more subtle in terms of a child's willingness to attempt something or their attitude towards learning. Nonetheless, some attempt should be made to evaluate what you did in order to inform yourself about the efficacy of an intervention.

Tips, ideas and activities
● Before evaluating an intervention you have made, ask your SENCO if there are already evaluation systems in place in.

● The first step is to consider the targets set and achieved. Identify targets that were achieved before the intervention and those that were achieved during it. Can you draw any conclusions about the value of the work that was done through this process? Does it look like the intervention has helped the child, or have the targets been achieved at the same rate that you would have expected without the intervention?

● Can you make any links to P scales or National Curriculum levels? Highlighting statements about the child's attainment before you begin the intervention and repeating the process at the end of it may give you useful information.

● Targets that are focused on self-esteem or motivation, rather than reading ability can be difficult to measure. Try asking the child questions before and after an intervention and recording the answer on a six-point scale.

● Record and celebrate all achievements, even those that are recorded as negatives: the target child hasn't prevented others from working, hasn't disrupted the class during story time, hasn't hidden their reading book more than once a week.

● Once you have gained some idea of the impact of the intervention on the target child, briefly consider what the options would have been. Would it have been better to: postpone any intervention; persuade colleagues who take an earlier class to put interventions in place; ask a teaching assistant to work with a small group rather than putting individual pressure on one child or work with an individual rather than a group?

● The intention of the evaluation is not to determine whether or not you are a caring teacher but simply that you can gain information to make informed decisions about future interventions.

Child's profile

Child's name: Today's date:
Date of birth: Home language:
Latest hearing test (date):   Result:
Latest vision test (date):   Result:
Brief description of concern:

Any history of speech and language therapy involvement?
Levels attained in:

reading _____   writing _____   maths _____

(Mark the following using the scale 6 = very good; 1 = very poor.)

— —

Can the child:

• Concentrate for an age-appropriate length of time at a self-chosen activity?

  6   5   4   3   2   1

• Concentrate for an age-appropriate length of time at a teacher-chosen activity?

  6   5   4   3   2   1

• Sustain listening to a story with pictures?

  6   5   4   3   2   1

• Sustain listening to a story without pictures?

  6   5   4   3   2   1

• Remember and follow an instruction with up to three parts?

  6   5   4   3   2   1

• Answer simple direct evidence questions about a text they have read?

  6   5   4   3   2   1

• Answer simple inferential questions about a text they have read?

  6   5   4   3   2   1

On the reverse of this sheet, ask the child to write their full name.

Phonological awareness MOT

Child's name: Date of birth: Date of MOT:

Look at the pictures. Can you name them? *(Slug, stamp, coin, beard.)*

1) Which word starts with *s-l*?

2) Which word has the sound *u*?

3) Which has the sound *oi*?

4) I'm going to say the sounds in a word: *c-oi-n*. What was the word?

5) Can you say all the sounds in this word? (Point to *stamp* then *beard*.)

6) Which picture shows the new word if I change the *j* in *join* to *c*?

7) Which picture shows the new word if I change the *e* in *bed* to *ear*?

8) Say *place*. Say it again without the *l*...; without the *p*...; without the *s*.

9) Which two of these words rhyme: *dot, dog, pot*?

10) Which two of these words begin with the same sound: *plate, pram, frog*?

11) Which two of these words have the same middle sound: *place, sheep, leaf?*

12) Tell me some words that begin with *ch*; that rhyme with *four*?

13) How much of the alphabet can you say?

14) Tell me the days of the week.

15) Tell me the months of the year.

16) Count backwards from 20.

Behaviours associated with dyslexia

This checklist should not be used as part of a diagnosis. It may be useful, however, for recording progress or as part of a request for further assessment.

Child's name: Date of birth: Date:

Is the child:

Clumsy?	☐ Yes	☐ No
Badly organised?	☐ Yes	☐ No
Forgetful?	☐ Yes	☐ No

Does the child:

Have neat handwriting?	☐ Yes	☐ No
Confuse the order of letters in a word? Words in a sentence?	☐ Yes	☐ No
Reverse letters and numbers? Ever mirror write?	☐ Yes	☐ No
Listen and concentrate well in class?	☐ Yes	☐ No
Have difficulty pronouncing multi-syllabic words?	☐ Yes	☐ No
Find it difficult to 'find' words to say?	☐ Yes	☐ No

Can the child:

Thread beads on a lace without dropping the lace or the beads?	☐ Yes	☐ No
Tie shoelaces?	☐ Yes	☐ No
Balance on one leg for five seconds?	☐ Yes	☐ No
Sequence the days of the week?	☐ Yes	☐ No
Sequence the alphabet?	☐ Yes	☐ No
Repeat four numbers in the opposite order from the order given?	☐ Yes	☐ No
Remember and follow a sequence of three instructions?	☐ Yes	☐ No
Say if two words rhyme? And give a list of rhyming words?	☐ Yes	☐ No
Tell you the sounds at the beginning and end of words?	☐ Yes	☐ No
Copy writing accurately?	☐ Yes	☐ No

Your child is

Gaining confidence in reading

When you have finished reading try:

- talking about the book. Ask questions like:
  - o *Who do you think were the good/bad characters?*
  - o *Why was the story set in that place?*
  - o *What else might have happened at the end?*

Give your child the chance to talk about other books they would like to read. Why not join the library?

Other activities you might enjoy together include:

- finding and learning favourite poems.
- helping your child to use non-fiction books to find out information for school projects.
- playing word games like *Scrabble* and *Boggle*.
- continuing to read aloud to your child.

4

You can help your child at home by:

- making sure that you read with them as often as possible – at least five times a week.

- making your reading time special and fun.

As you read the book with your child:

   o you can read alternate pages. This helps your child to hear what fluent reading sounds like.

   o encourage them to use some expression.

   o comment on what is happening in the story.

   o congratulate them on their reading.

If they get stuck:

   o ask what they think the word might be.

   o ask what they can do to work out the word.

   o help them to recognise tricky bits in words.

   o tell them the word. Don't spend too long over each word.

3

Your child is...

Reading with confidence

This means that they:

- read longer books which may not have a picture on every page.

- need to glance through a book before they begin to read it.

- are able to use all of the letters in a word when they are sounding out, including where two or more letters represent one sound (*b-r-ea-d, l-igh-t*).

- can also use the meaning of a sentence to work words out.

- should stop and correct themselves if they make a mistake.

- are using some expression when they are reading.

2

Your child is

An independent reader

When your child has finished reading a book:

- talk about the book:
  - o Did it live up to expectations?
  - o What happened in the book?
  - o What were its strengths? And weaknesses?
  - o Would they recommend the book to their friends? Why? Why not?

- try to extend the range of books your child reads.

- find and learn favourite poems.

- use non-fiction books and the internet to find information for school projects.

- play word games like *Scrabble* and *Boggle*.

- continue to read aloud to your child.

4

You can help your child at home by:

- encouraging them to read five times a week.
- making time to read with them.

Help your child to select the right book. Ask them:

- why they have chosen this book. Do they know the author? Do they like the genre (the type of book)? Did they find the blurb interesting?
- to do the five finger test with the first page of the text. They should read the page aloud. Every time they get stuck on a word, they should hold up one finger. If they hold up five fingers on the first page, the book is probably too hard for them to read independently.

As your child reads the book:

- o you can read alternate pages or paragraphs. This helps your child to hear what fluent reading sounds like.
- o let them read parts of the book to themselves.
- o ask them to summarise each section or chapter.

3

Your child is...

An independent reader

This means that they:

- are able to read longer books which may have some black and white pictures or no pictures at all.
- need to glance through a book before they begin to read it.
- are able to use syllables and their knowledge of word patterns to help to identify words they don't know.
- can also use the meaning of a sentence to work words out.
- should stop and correct themselves if they make a mistake.
- may like to read quietly to themselves.

2

Index

SCHOLASTIC

Also available in this series:

ISBN 978-1407-10173-6

ISBN 978-1407-10174-3

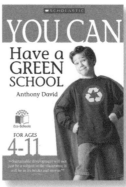
ISBN 978-1407-10083-8

ISBN 978-1407-10070-8

ISBN 978-0439-94534-9

ISBN 978-0439-94535-6

ISBN 978-0439-96522-4

ISBN 978-0439-96523-1

ISBN 978-0439-96534-7

ISBN 978-0439-96539-2

ISBN 978-0439-96540-8

ISBN 978-0439-96554-5

ISBN 978-0439-96555-2

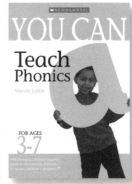
ISBN 978-0439-94554-7

ISBN 978-0439-94530-1

ISBN 978-0439-94531-8

ISBN 978-0439-94532-5

ISBN 978-0439-94533-2

ISBN 978-0439-94559-2

To find out more, call: 0845 603 9091
or visit our website www.scholastic.co.uk